Mary,

Thanks for your leadership in the selection process. It is fun to work with other innovative firms and people. We look forward to collaborating in 2010 and beyond.

Best regards.

Dave G

UNBOUND

HOW ENTREPRENEURSHIP IS DRAMATICALLY TRANSFORMING LEGAL SERVICES TODAY

by

DAVID J. GALBENSKI

written with

DAVID BARRINGER

2009

"A pessimist sees the difficulty in every opportunity. An optimist sees the opportunity in every difficulty."

—Sir Winston Churchill (1874–1965),
British Prime Minister during World War II

CONTENTS

After the Fire

Introduction

The financial and economic crisis of 2008 delivered the final blow to any skeptics still resisting change in the legal industry. The legal industry is now rushing toward dramatic transformation. Change is long overdue. I have been in the legal staffing and consulting industry for over fifteen years, and I have witnessed dynamic change both in this industry and in related industries. Over the next three to five years, the legal landscape will be dramatically reshaped. Law will continue on its global march. Even small firms are outsourcing legal support work overseas. Large firms are consolidating into even larger firms. Many will adapt or merge or scramble to survive in small niches. Many will simply go out of business. All will have to acknowledge the forces that are reshaping this industry, and they will have to make serious decisions that go to the heart of how they do business.

The Purpose of This Book

I hope this book will inspire readers to think in new ways about law and business. As an entrepreneur, I am excited by today's trends and what they promise for the future. The legal industry is becoming unbound from its limitations. It is flexing its muscles and expanding its vision. Those individuals who are currently highly successful in the legal industry might have cause to be ambivalent about the pressures of the business model on their profession. But they also have good reason to become more alert to global as well as business trends and to seize the opportunity to adapt, innovate and thrive in the changing environment.

Why Me

I have been running a legal staffing and consulting company since 1993. For years, I have witnessed the dynamics impacting the legal industry. I have had to react to these changes for the continual improvement of my business, and I have made it my job to pay attention to industry trends nationally and globally. Because entrepreneurship has always been a passion for me, I joined the global Entrepreneurs' Organization (EO) in 1999. Hailing from thirty-eight countries, the EO's 7,000 members have an average age of thirty-eight and run companies generating an average $15 million a year in revenue. As an EO member, I traveled the globe meeting entrepreneurs, lawyers, and government officials. Listening to their experiences and visiting their countries, I received a firsthand perspective on the global economic transformation. I have been fortunate enough to visit Australia, Canada, China, Dominican Republic, England, Germany, India, Japan, Mexico, Morocco, Portugal, Russia, Saudi Arabia, Singapore, Spain, Sri Lanka, Switzerland, and United Arab Emirates. I served as EO chairman in 2008 to 2009.

What This Book is About

I have synthesized information about several trends affecting the legal industry. Journalists and industry researchers have been describing the current state of these trends for years now, but I wanted to encapsulate the importance of all these trends into a single book. I wanted especially to draw the reader's attention to where these trends might be going. In light of these trends and the current economic crisis facing the globe, those in the industry will need to revisit their three- to five-year business plans to remain relevant in the industry.

The Interviews

I am not the only one thinking about the future, and I certainly do not pretend to possess a crystal ball. So I knew it was critical to include the perspectives of other industry leaders. From September 2008 to

February 2009, just as the economic crisis was roaring through the U.S. and the world, I conducted up-to-the-minute interviews with industry leaders and legal visionaries. I asked them how they were responding to trends in legal services, including globalization, technology, staffing, compensation, performance metrics, recruiting, and more. As general counsel, outside counsel, and legal entrepreneurs, they reveal what it is like for them to respond to the urgencies of today while they keep their eyes on the trends sure to affect them tomorrow.

The Forces Affecting the Legal Industry

The forces affecting the legal industry derive in part from the convergence of business, law and entrepreneurship. Business insists on efficiency. As the practice of law opens up to business demands, entrepreneurs can seize upon new opportunities. Entrepreneurs, both inside and outside the industry, will think creatively and design new models. They will take risks and make investments. They will do what entrepreneurs in every industry try to do: deliver services better, faster and cheaper.

The Fire

I had been working on this book for almost two years when, in late 2008, global stock markets lost $3.1 trillion in four days, and the Dow Jones Industrial

Average fell below 10,000 for the first time in five years.

The bubble in the housing market had burst. Home foreclosures were at historic levels. The news media could barely keep up with the torrent of bad news arriving beneath the waves of financial jargon: "subprime mortgages," "toxic derivatives," "mortgage-backed securities," "collateralized debt obligations." Google's top economic searches in 2008 included: "financial crisis," "depression," "bailout," "mortgage crisis," "subprime," "credit crisis," and "housing crisis." People were confused and desperate for answers. A year of recession was taking its toll. World markets were shaken. Financial giants like Lehman Brothers and Washington Mutual went bankrupt. Others were on the verge of bankruptcy. The U.S. government took over Fannie Mae and Freddie Mac and debated the terms of a $700-billion bailout for the financial and banking industry. Automotive companies sought government loans. Established retail franchises were closing stores or going out of business altogether.

In January 2009, the Bureau of Labor Statistics of the U.S. Department of Labor reported its findings for the year ending December 2008. The unemployment rate had risen to 7.2%. In a year, the number of unemployed people in the U.S. had grown by 3.6 million to 11.1 million. In the month of December alone, 632,000 people had lost their jobs. And the fire continued into January 2009. In the last week of January, even after news of the $825-billion stimulus bill proposed by U.S. Congressional House Democrats and U.S. President Barack Obama, American companies—including Caterpillar, Kodak, Home Depot, IBM, and Microsoft—announced 65,000 layoffs.

As for the legal industry, 7,000 jobs were lost in 2008, according to the U.S. Department of Labor. The big law firms laid off 1,762 lawyers, associates and staff in all of 2008, but then laid off an astounding 1,528 people in January 2009 alone. Goodrich & Rosati laid off 45 lawyers and 68 staff. Cooley Godward Kronish laid off 52 lawyers and 62 staff. Clifford Chance laid off over 70 associates in their London office. Morrison & Foerster laid off 53 lawyers and 148 staff. On January 29, *Bloomberg* reported that Linklaters, the second-largest law firm in London with 2,644 lawyers in twenty-seven countries, was planning to lay off 120 salaried lawyers and as many as 150 staff. In 2008, Linklaters had already laid off 125 of its lawyers in eastern Europe. (Ongoing layoff trackers can be found at LawShucks.com, AbovetheLaw.com, the *Wall Street Journal*'s Law Blog, and the *American Lawyer*'s Layoff List.) At the end of January, the 130-year-old law firm Fish & Richardson, whose 500 lawyers practice litigation, intellectual property, and corporate law, released a statement to the press that captured the bottom-line desperation of the time:

The global recession has profoundly impacted many businesses, and many of our clients have reduced spending on legal services. Faced with unprecedented levels of economic uncertainty and an attorney attrition rate that is significantly below normal levels, we have adjusted our staffing to meet our clients' changing business needs. We have reduced our workforce after strategically evaluating our projected needs in all of our practice groups. As a result:

—Since November of last year, 49 members of our legal staff have left or are in the process of leaving the firm, including four dismissals that were made today, January 30, 2009. Many of these departures occurred as the result of year-end performance evaluations, but others were based on purely economic decisions.

—Thirty employees of our support staff across eight of our U.S. offices in several administrative departments were asked to leave the firm on January 28, 2009.

[Courtesy of AbovetheLaw.com]

Like many people, I was overwhelmed by the scope and depth of the crisis. There were daily reports of shocking new developments, from Bank of America's buyout of Merrill Lynch to the bankruptcy of Iceland to the $50-billion hedge-fund Ponzi scheme of Bernard Madoff, a former NASDAQ chairman. The bad news kept coming from the legal industry as well. On March 4, *The National Law Journal* reported that major U.S. law firms were laying off attorneys and staff not in the dozens but in the hundreds. Dewey & LeBoeuf laid off 100 staff. O'Melveny & Meyers laid off 90 attorneys and 110 staff. Orrick Herrington & Sutcliffe laid off 100 attorneys and 200 staff. As global chairman of the Entrepreneurs' Organization, I was called upon to give speeches during this time, and the economic crisis was an unavoidable topic. I had to come up with a shorthand way to talk about it.

I decided on fire.

My family and I had vacationed in Yellowstone Park in July of 2008, and we learned about the historic Yellowstone Fire of 1988. That year, the forest was in serious drought. A single spark might have been enough to start a fire, and on June 14, 1988, one started in Storm Creek. Most forest fires burn out after consuming an acre. This one was different. Flames reached as high as 200 feet. Winds blew at 80 miles per hour. Wildlife fled as the blaze burned in a mosaic pattern. Firefighters attacked from the ground and from the air, in helicopters and planes. This continued for months. The focus of the efforts changed from extinguishing the flames to limiting the damage. Tens of millions of trees were lost. Many were hundreds of years old. It cost $120 million and took 25,000 people to fight the fire and to protect people and property. Mother Nature finally contained the fire with a snowfall. The last flames burned out for good on November 18, 1988. Of the 2.2 million acres of Yellowstone, 800,000 had burned.

After the Fire

Media reports exaggerated the impact of the catastrophe. Some predicted the death of the park. While many lodgepole trees, some over 200 years old and 130 feet high, had burned and died, their seeds had been released in the fire's extreme heat. New seeds took root in the ash. Birds returned to nest in dead trees. Wildflowers sprouted in the enriched soil.

My family and I learned about Yellowstone's recovery from watching a 1998 documentary, shown during our visit. Already, only ten years after the fire, new lodgepole trees dominated the landscape, rising gradually from a horizon that had been leveled by the blaze. By the time of our visit in 2008, twenty years had passed, and if we had not seen that documentary, we would never have guessed that a wildfire had done so much damage. For us, it was summer in Yellowstone: green, lush, and vibrant.

A few months after our visit, I realized the park's recovery from disaster could provide an optimistic analogy for the world's economic crisis. Nature's resilience could be instructive. It could counteract all the overheated talk of doomsday and give us a cooler perspective based on reason and hope.

I do not want to push the analogy too far, but it is tempting to see in those old lodgepole trees the embodiments of *The National Law Journal*'s top 250 law firms. As the economic crisis spreads, old firms topple, and partners flee. Reports of the death of the law firm are greatly exaggerated, but the fire of the crisis still burns. The global landscape changes every day. We are trying to limit the damage and protect ourselves. The last ember will one day fade beneath an icy layer of snow. The scorched earth will cool. Already, there is opportunity in the ashes. Seeds are taking root.

The Seven Trends

Vigilance

I have identified seven major trends that I believe will greatly affect the industry in the next three to five years. I know what I have seen and experienced over the last fifteen years, both in my business and as an active member and chairman of the Entrepreneurs' Organization, but I also know full well that the future is up for grabs. As a participant in this market, I have to take stock continually of what forces are putting pressure locally, nationally and globally on the practice of law and the provision of legal services. This vigilance about the marketplace is an essential feature of successful entrepreneurship. I am not the only one who feels this pressure to be vigilant about the marketplace. The legal industry is changing in dramatic, visible ways, and it seems common sense to pay attention now rather than later.

The Seven Summarized

From the provider's point of view, the trends are affecting how we organize, value, and provide legal services, how we relate to competitors and vendors, and whom we employ.

From the consumer's point of view, the trends are affecting what they know about legal services, how they buy legal services, and from whom they buy.

Here is a short rundown of the trends.

1 | There will be new ways *to buy* legal services.

The demands of business to provide services better, faster and cheaper are forcing the legal industry to behave less like a profession and more like a business.

2 | There will be new ways *to provide* legal services.

Globalization is the force that will expand the ways in which legal services are provided to the end consumer.

3 | There will be new ways *to organize* legal services.

Tasks will become unbundled, both as a result of business pressures but also as a result of globalization.

4 | Legal-service providers will feel more pressure *to consolidate.*

This consolidation trend will be the result of the new global scale of conducting business. Go global or go niche.

5 | There will be new ways *to know* about legal services.

Consumers and clients know more about legal services than ever before. Information is more available, and the industry is more transparent. This is the self-help trend.

6 | New categories and types of people will be called upon *to perform* legal services.

The demographic composition of the workforce and the attitudes of those working are changing. This is the people trend.

7 | There will be new ways *to educate* legal professionals.

Legal education will have to respond to these changing dynamics as law schools prepare the next generation of legal professionals for the new ways legal services are organized and delivered.

One

The Better/Faster/Cheaper Trend

New ways to buy legal services

The vast majority of work performed by lawyers is billed by the hour, and they bill the same hourly rate for every task. This has been a boon for the profession for decades.

A changing marketplace, however, is forcing the legal industry to behave less like a profession and more like a business. The transition began in the 1980s and continues today. Law is entrenched within a professional model, and this is understandable. Many firms have been around for more than a hundred years. So even with the pressures of the last twenty years, law firms still bill the vast majority of their work using the premium pricing of the hourly rate. It's hard to give up a good thing.

But they are going to have to change and give up this good thing, if they want to survive.

For the next few years, most law firms will continue to dig in their heels against the pressure to change the way they bill for their services. So the changes will start at the bottom of the pricing continuum.

The fall of the billable hour and of premium pricing will begin with a crumbling at the lowest tier of services, represented by those tasks susceptible to unbundling, standardization, and outsourcing. These are the tasks typically done by paralegals and junior associates but billed at an inflated hourly rate. Document review is a good example. Patent application is another good example. This and many other kinds of work are already being outsourced to contract staff, third-party vendors, and even overseas legal professionals. Law firms are being forced to consider the economic benefits of outsourcing low-level tasks for a simple reason: their clients are demanding it.

Corporations want to control their operating costs, and legal services are regarded as operating costs. So corporations are setting their sights on legal services as targets for increasing efficiency. Law firms are now engaged in competitive bidding, just like players in every other service industry. As clients focus on efficiency and learn more about the workings of legal services, legal-service providers will have to let go of their good thing. They will have to establish more efficient internal rate structures for low-end tasks.

Most significantly for the future, the new pricing structures will move upstream in the value chain of tasks, especially those tasks that can be unbundled and standardized. In other words, once the crumbling starts at the bottom, it is bound to move up.

The pressure to change has intensified in reaction to the economic crisis. "This is the time to get rid of the billable hour," said Evan R. Chesler, presiding partner at Cravath Swaine & Moore in New York, in an article in the *New York Times*, January 29, 2009. "Clients are concerned about the budgets, more so than perhaps a year or two ago."

Indeed, the consulting firm Altman Weil surveyed 115 general counsel in November 2008 and found that 75% were facing budget cuts for 2009. The top concerns for general counsel were, in order of importance: outside-counsel costs, the unpredictability of legal spending, the inefficiency of the billable-hour model, litigation risk, and budget pressure from corporate executives. Strategies for reducing costs included bringing more work in-house, moving work to more affordable outside counsel, increasing the utilization of contract lawyers, demanding more alternative fees (83% of general counsel surveyed still rely on hourly billing almost exclusively), cutting spending on training and special events, sending work overseas, thinning staff, and reducing compensation.

From 2001 to 2007, law firms saw double-digit growth in revenue and partner profits almost every year, a dynamic driven by the ability of law firms to simply raise rates year after year. But in 2008, law firms saw a decline in average partner profits, and they will see a greater decline in 2009. According to a client advisory from Hildebrandt and Citi Private Bank, issued in February 2009, profits-per-partner stayed the same or decreased by as much as 10% from 2007 to 2008, and 2009 profits are expected to decline more severely, from 5–15%. Desperate to cut costs, law firms have begun to reduce bonuses, freeze associate salaries, lay off staff, push underperforming partners out, and experiment with alternative compensation structures. Expenses will continue to rise, credit will remain tight, and the demand for legal services will continue to shrink.

"We now expect the global economy to come to a virtual halt," said Olivier Blanchard, chief economist of the International Monetary Fund (IMF), who spoke during a press conference at the end of January 2009. On January 28, the IMF had released updates to its *World Economic Outlook* and *Global Financial Stability Report*. The IMF projected world economic growth to fall to 0.5% for 2009, the lowest rate in sixty years. The IMF also changed its estimate of the potential loss in value of U.S.-originated credit assets that were held by banks and other institutions. In October 2008, the IMF estimated the loss to be $1.4 trillion. In January 2009, they changed their estimate to $2.2 trillion.

The global recession challenges every industry, and the legal industry is no exception. Having been dependent for so long on hourly-rate increases for profitability, law firms are handicapped as they confront an already difficult challenge. They need to develop (and invest in the implementation of) innovative strategies for thoroughly revamping their business models. And it is going to be very hard for

LAYOFFS IN BIG FIRMS

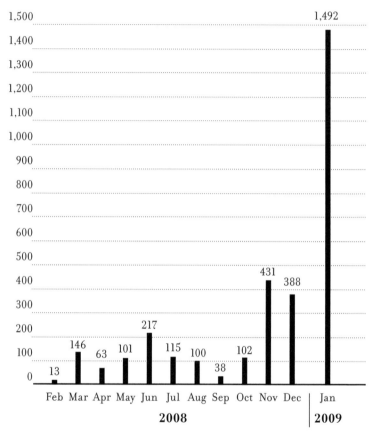

Source: Layoff numbers include partners, associates, and staff of larger law firms as collected by LawShucks.com. See graph, page 79.

them to build a new ship when the leaky ship they are in is being tossed by a hurricane.

"The big message is that it's going to be a bit of a bumpy ride," said James Jones, a vice president of Hildebrandt International, quoted in *The National Law Journal* on February 3, 2009. "But it's an opportunity to do things that probably should have been done before."

Nine days later, on February 12, 2009, law firms across the country laid off nearly 800 associates and legal staff in one day.

Two other forces should be noted here. The first is a management trend, that of an increasing focus on metrics. Corporate legal departments are starting to use metrics to increase efficiency and to benchmark law-firm performance. Our interview subjects have a lot to say about this issue, and I address the trend in the chapter "What Are You Doing? What Should You Be Doing?"

The second is an unsustainable salary trend. Typically, the top firms lure top law-school graduates with high first-year salaries. This is the dynamic that maintains the firm's rationale for billing premium hourly rates. They have the top lawyers, so they charge the most. In response, competitive firms raise their salaries. As the effects of business pressures are felt more keenly, however, none but the top firms will be able to sustain this model. Most other firms will have to change their model, their pricing, and their competitive strategies, or risk collapse. In early 2009, we are seeing law firms question lock-step associate advancement and compensation and finally taking seriously those models based on competence and performance.

"There are other models, like virtual law firms, whereby lawyers contract a certain number of hours each month. There is no overhead in real estate. The virtual law firm relies on contract staff leveraged by information and communication technology."

PAUL SMITH, *Partner*
EVERSHEDS
LONDON, UK

INTERVIEW...

What is Eversheds?

Eversheds is a full-service law firm with a staff of 5,000 people, half of whom are attorneys. We deal with matters in sixty countries. We don't have an office in the U.S., however, because we've taken the view that you have plenty of attorneys in the U.S. We serve 500 U.S. corporations by supporting them internationally, which allows them to continue their relationships with U.S. firms while expanding globally. We manage risk and control cost. We are client-centered and international, and we enter into deep partnering relationships.

How has the financial crisis affected the legal industry?

Everyone is feeling the pain. I'm hearing from general counsel that they're now being asked to forecast and set fixed budgets to meet their legal needs, no matter what litigation is around the corner.

Will there be greater pressure now to create alternatives to the billable hour?

We've been pioneers for over ten years now of alternative fees, and it's a bit surprising that ninety percent of the general counsel we survey expect the hourly rate to remain in place during the lifetime of their careers. We've identified twenty-two different alternative-fee mechanisms within Eversheds. I've been on the lecture circuit in the U.S. talking about what we've been doing overseas, and the response is, "Why aren't U.S. firms doing this?" The fact is there is huge resistance to change from both U.S. general counsel and law firms. This increased pressure on costs and budgets might at long last force firms and general counsel to look at other ways to share risk and reward, which is what alternative fees are all about.

What do general counsel say about alternative fees?

When general counsel talk to me, they say alternative fees sound fine, but they often don't have the ability to analyze whether or not they're getting a good deal with alternative-fee mechanisms. And I say we'll get the finance people involved very early in the process. Some clients have their own finance people deal with our finance people to reach an understanding about the pricing model. This requires trust and partnering.

How has globalization affected the job of general counsel?

More U.S. corporations are looking overseas for new business, and their legal resources are often based in the U.S. with little on the ground in new countries. It's difficult for general counsel to know which firms to hire and how to negotiate fees in other countries.

Greater regulation is another concern. More regulation of
businesses internationally will increase the scope and
complexity for general counsel advising corporations of
the new laws and liabilities around the world.

General counsel are increasingly business managers.
They are expected to have management skills and to
advise the company on business issues. Law firms are
very fearful of changing the model, because that's what
everyone has grown up with, especially in the U.S. where
compensation is designed to rack up hours and bills and
where you eat what you kill. We recognized this a few
years ago, that the compensation model in firms, when
simply based on how much you bill for your clients, is
not conducive for building relationships. We have the
agility to enter into long-term relationships with clients
such as Tyco, DuPont, and Boeing.

What about U.S. firms expanding globally?

Over the last couple years, U.S. firms have ramped up
their efforts to have an international offering. But the
difficulty is that when you come head to head, you really
need local lawyers on the ground to be effective. Some
U.S. firms, like Baker & McKenzie, have been doing this
for years already.

Will firms consolidate to better provide global solutions for international clients?

For many years, I have held the belief that we would
become a one-stop shop for legal services, and critics
said it was impossible. But Tyco pushed us to provide
one-stop international service. We created an integrated
billing service that covers up to sixty countries with a
standardized, online system. The client gets one bill
in U.S. dollars, no matter where the work happens

overseas. It wasn't easy getting lawyers in so many different jurisdictions and cultures to understand and participate. But we've been through the pain barrier. We call the network the Global Account Management system (GAM). Other firms claim to be creating something similar to play catch up. But it will be difficult. Most of the good firms out there have already been taken over or merged. If I had a blank sheet and had to do it now, I'd look for spinoffs from big firms in other countries looking to have an international presence.

Why was it difficult to get lawyers and firms in other countries to agree to this standardized international system?
We're very big into project management, budgets, and analysis, but in Turkey, Greece and many other countries, that's never been the way law has been practiced. I had a discussion with a senior partner from a law firm serving a Central European company, and we talked about the 21st century law firm, and he said they're not even in the 19th century. Those who get it and fight their way through it, however, enjoy an unintended consequence. Because of their advances into the new model, they now have access to many more clients. So once they've gone through the pain of adapting, they pass a threshold, and new clients open up to them.

What demographic trends are affecting you now?
The biggest trend I see is the generational change. My generation, the Baby Boomers, will retire over the next several years, and if you've read any studies, Generations X and Y are entirely different in how they see the world. Their motivations and lifestyle choices are different. We aspired to the pyramid model of law firms, with partners at the apex, whereas the younger generations value their lives outside the firm.

What will the future of legal services look like?
The Legal Transformation Study suggests four scenarios for
the future of legal services: consolidation, automation,
the proliferation of experts, and an e-marketplace.
When the Study came out in March of 2008, the most
popular scenario was one of global consolidation, that
eight large international law firms will dominate the
market like the accountancy firms do. The e-marketplace
was a vision of a variety of suppliers: law firms, service
providers, insurance companies, banks, and other
providers offering quasi-legal services. Online legal
networking sites are another part of this.

What other trends do you see developing in the future?
There are other models, like virtual law firms, whereby
lawyers contract a certain number of hours each month.
The firm operates virtually. There is no overhead in real
estate. The virtual law firm relies on contract staff leveraged by information and communication technology. In
2012, the cityscape may look radically different. There
may be lots of green parks and landscapes and even small
farms, because no one will need to come to a centralized
office building to work. We took part in a teleconfer-
ence with Cisco, and we were in a room in which half
the room was real, and the other half was a video screen
showing an identical set of table and chairs on the other
side of the world. Baby Boomers will retire and leave
their pyramid models and their big offices, and the next
generation will move toward a far more flexible model.
Several scenarios may happen in concert or at odds.

Two

The Globalization Trend

New ways to provide legal services

Globalization is the force that will expand the ways in which legal services are provided to the end consumer.

It is simply a different world from even ten years ago. Advances in communications technology have changed the way people do business. We talk on mobile phones or via Skype to people on the other side of the world. We send documents by email. We collaborate using web-based software. We work in virtual offices and virtual war rooms. Other countries suddenly open to international business expand the pool of labor and the market for goods and services, and this affects not only the global economy, but your ability to hire someone in India, Israel or the Philippines for document review.

The legal industry's time has come. The forces affecting the legal industry are the same that have already affected—and continue to affect—other service and professional industries. It is old news that manufacturing moves toward cheap labor, from the U.S. to Mexico, Korea, China, and Vietnam. And now it's old news that service industries, like customer service, tech support, financial services, and even accounting services, have built facilities overseas in countries like India, Indonesia, and Australia. Each of these moves caused an uproar at the time. Change is always risky, and you cannot always predict the effects. When you call customer service for your computer, you are likely to talk to someone in India, where Dell or Hewlett-Packard has built a call center. Now it is also likely that someone overseas has performed some task related to your credit-card account or your investment portfolio. Citibank and Fidelity Investments have overseas facilities, as do many accounting companies. Reasonable concerns about security, privacy, efficiency, and even consumer reaction have been addressed. What was once unthinkable is now familiar. And the legal industry is next.

The globalization of legal services is the most dramatic force affecting the legal industry. Globalization of labor and services, of information and technology, affects the who, the what, the where, and the when of the business of law. The old picture of a solitary lawyer toiling away in an oak-paneled library has given way to the new picture of a connected lawyer. The new lawyer is connected to the world by telephone, internet, and email. There are offices in Cleveland, New York, and New Delhi. Your partner is down the hall, but your paralegal is down under in Australia, and your law clerks are in Hyderabad, India. It is an expansion, first, of the imagination. You have to conceive of your work in a global dimension. Legal providers are using global resources to serve their clients. They are not thinking nationally. They are working globally.

Globalization is putting pressure on U.S. law in unexpected ways. General counsel of national companies have to advise their clients on the laws of many different states. State laws can vary significantly, and general counsel cannot pass the bar exam and earn a license to practice in each and every state. Through research and the use of outside counsel, general counsel have to attempt to get a handle on a variety of regulatory environments. In the end, they have to advise their clients.

Now take this national situation and extrapolate it internationally. Again, through reliance on in-house attorneys, legal research, and outside counsel, the general counsel can try to get a grip on the rules and regulations of various countries around the world. In the end, they have to advise their clients. To define this challenge as difficult understates the case.

Both the national and international situations are calling existing licensing systems and even legal systems into question. Will the practice of law become national in the U.S., at least in certain practice areas or industry regulatory systems? Will a new kind of national license to practice be offered, in addition to state licenses? If a general counsel can advise a corporate client on regulations and laws in states and, indeed, in countries in which the counsel does not hold a license to practice law, then can attorneys from outside the U.S. assume the roles of general counsel for U.S.-based international corporations?

"More U.S.-based companies' senior in-house positions are going to non-U.S. lawyers," observed Don Liu, general counsel of Xerox, in his interview following this section. "Fifty-three percent of Xerox's revenues and related legal work is not based solely on U.S. law. I don't see why a non-U.S. attorney at some point in the future couldn't do my job, again subject to resolution of licensing issues. I'm aware of at least two U.S. public companies that had a non-U.S. lawyer who ran their legal department, although they couldn't call themselves the general counsel because of licensing requirements."

The legal industry and its systems of laws and regulations will be under pressure from the increasing globalization of large corporations. Companies are trying to reach consumers all over the U.S. and the world. General counsel have to respond to the demands for national and international legal advice, identify risk, and help their clients navigate the complex legal landscapes from Texas to Tokyo. As the economic downturn continues to pressure the legal industry, there may be new pressures on certain regulatory systems to nationalize, as unlikely as that may seem, given how embedded the state licensing system is in the U.S. Still, in-house attorneys may find general-counsel positions going to more non-U.S. attorneys the more that corporate clients expand their global reach and their corresponding need for global legal advice.

Globalization also affects how providers reduce expenses inside the business. More corporate law departments are hiring operating officers and dedicated managers to complement the general counsel, and now more law firms are hiring full-time CEOs. They have decided it is better to have a CEO devoted solely to business operations rather than rely on a managing partner/CEO who balances a practice workload with the demands of running the firm. The result is an acceleration of efficiency efforts. Once the leadership is comfortable using global resources to reduce expenses at the lowest levels by, say, outsourcing document review, then it follows that the efforts will move up the value chain. The focus will shift to reducing expenses at the next levels.

There is more. Large firms will continue to open overseas offices and merge with overseas firms. Nine major U.S. law firms (of those included in the *NLJ* 250) merged with overseas firms in 2007 and 2008. The overseas firms were located in London, Paris, Madrid, Dusseldorf, Frankfurt, Tokyo, Taipei, and Hong Kong. *The National Law Journal* has been tracking the rising number of overseas offices opened by the *NLJ* 250 law firms, from 148 offices in 1987 to 368 in 1997 to 551 in 2007.

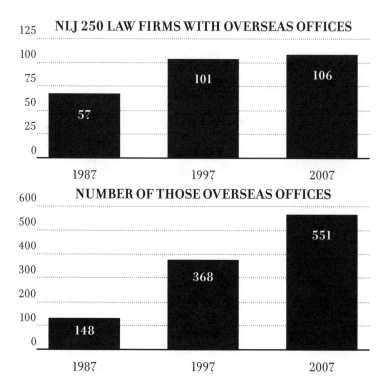

NLJ 250 LAW FIRMS WITH OVERSEAS OFFICES

57	101	106
1987	1997	2007

NUMBER OF THOSE OVERSEAS OFFICES

148	368	551
1987	1997	2007

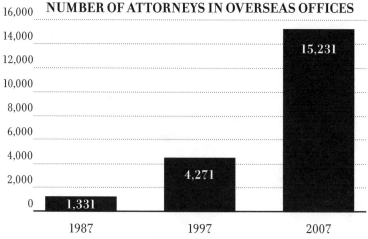

NUMBER OF ATTORNEYS IN OVERSEAS OFFICES

1,331	4,271	15,231
1987	1997	2007

Source: Information on the numbers of *NLJ* 250 law firms with overseas offices and overseas attorneys from *The National Law Journal*.

And there is room for much more growth (at least for the largest law firms). The *NLJ* 250 represented 128,213 lawyers in 2007, which means 15,231 overseas lawyers represented only 12% of that total. Law firms are considered to be global when they have at least 25% of their lawyers overseas.

India has banned foreign law firms since 1995, but in January 2009, *Bloomberg* reported that the Indian government was circulating a draft of new regulations for opening their legal market. Sure enough, in February, India enacted the Limited Liability Partnership Act, Section 59 of which allows foreign law firms to establish a place of business—but not to practice law—in India. Once India and other countries completely open their doors to foreign-owned law firms, firms will build offices there (if they have not already by that time) and employ local lawyers directly. I predict the legal market will open up in this way no later than 2012. Imagine this. Legal-process outsourcing is right now a $4 billion industry. Imagine how firms within India will alter the legal landscape. The entire industry could be captured and delivered by totally different firms than those providing these services today!

"Those companies only focused on counting heads . . . are not focused on the right issue. You can reduce heads, but you may often increase total legal cost by being forced to send work to outside firms."

DON LIU, *Corporate Senior Vice President and General Counsel*
XEROX CORPORATION
NORWALK, CT

INTERVIEW..

What are the pressures on you as general counsel today?
We are trying to improve the quality of performance and
   the efficiency of our legal department and outside
   counsel. This is a bigger challenge in a recessionary
   period. But whether we're talking about good or bad
   times, the long-term trend is that companies are
   increasingly looking to general counsel for efficiencies
   in their legal departments. During my career, I've
   been in four legal departments across four industries.
   And a key component of the role of every general-
   counsel position I had has been to control cost. For the
   foreseeable future, I think this will be the case.

How do you respond to this pressure to control cost?
I've considered and used different methods. In my view,
   those companies that are only focused on counting heads
   (i.e., the number of in-house lawyers) are not focused
   on the right issue. You can reduce heads, but you may

often increase total legal cost by being forced to send work to outside firms. I have often used insourcing as a way to control costs, which is sometimes more cost-effective than outsourcing. So the methods that are applied depend somewhat on the metrics that the Chief Financial Officer chooses to use for judging efficiencies at the company.

The goal is to use the right tools and methods that address the unique circumstances and meet the specific needs of the company. One example is the use of temporary attorneys. Temporary agencies have grown because the strategy of reducing in-house lawyers naturally increases the need for outsourcing legal work and because certain short-term legal work can be more efficiently performed by temporary attorneys. I've used them to replace staff on maternity leave and sometimes during extremely busy periods. I've also used temporary staff when we've had unusual projects and needed special outside expertise that could have been performed by law firms at a higher cost.

The point is that there is no magic bullet. Finding the right tool for the specific challenge is the key.

Are you using performance metrics to help you decide how to coordinate the work?
Yes, but statistics need to be used for the right purpose, and proper use of them requires judgment. Some people are looking for the Holy Grail in relying upon statistics, but not every case or legal issue is alike. In litigation, you can spend $500,000 on one matter and $100,000 on a similar matter, but the comparative dollars spent on those matters may not reflect efficiencies because the lawsuits may be very different.

The trend to utilize data in the practice of law is stronger today than when I started legal practice. It's a good trend. Law firms are increasingly using these data and are also being asked for data by their clients. The use of electronic billing is increasing and becoming standardized. Eventually, I think there will be two or three standard electronic-billing systems.

We do look at statistics to assess efficiencies, like how much we are spending from the start to the finish of a project. We look at which firms are taking longer and costing more. We look at the average rate per associate versus the partner rate. You could have a ten-percent lower rate from one lawyer to another, but the cheaper one may be half as productive. We look at diversity statistics, although there is some subjectivity there. What looks great in Iowa may not look great in New York, considering the different demographics.

How does globalization affect you?
Globalization is real and here to stay. Global growth is often more important for larger companies, as it presents greater growth opportunities than the domestic market. In the short- to mid-term, revenue growth for Xerox is expected to be higher overseas than in the U.S. That will impact how we provide legal services considerably. If overseas revenues grow faster than U.S. revenues, that means my legal needs will grow more overseas than here. It also means we'll have increased cross-border legal needs. Globalization often raises legal issues involving multiple countries. For these needs, we won't necessarily cross borders to look for talent. Sometimes, we just need attorneys who are comfortable dealing with multinational transactions and legal disputes.

How do you deal with issues that cross borders?

Let's assume we're dealing with a transaction involving
four countries: the U.S., the UK, and some services
performed in two other countries. The U.S. in-house
lawyer who is working on the transaction will need to
understand the UK law as well as the laws in the two
other countries. We generally have a hard time finding
law firms that will have all four countries covered. So we
consider using multiple firms to address the legal issues
arising in those countries. Even if one law firm were able
to cover those four countries, the firm may not have local
experts with knowledge of the specific laws needed for
the transaction. That will often lead to a need to look for
local counsel in those places.

It's not easy to manage this process. It's also not easy for a
U.S. lawyer to judge and measure the performance of an
outside firm in a foreign country. How does a U.S. lawyer
judge a lawyer in Kazakhstan, for example? You can
apply some U.S. tools to evaluate, but you are very often
dealing with apples and oranges. Still, you don't have
many alternatives. In the end, it's like anything else in
life. You do this stuff often enough, and you will become
more comfortable and familiar with the process. Having
attorneys who are experienced and comfortable with
unfamiliar cultures becomes increasingly important.

**With the rise of this globalized practice of law, will
general counsel in the U.S. compete with non-U.S.
attorneys for their jobs?**

Subject to resolving the current attorney-license
requirements under state laws, I believe that is
inevitable. More U.S.-based companies' senior in-house
positions are going to non-U.S. lawyers. Fifty-three
percent of Xerox's revenues and related legal work is

not based solely on U.S. law. I don't see why a non-U.S. attorney at some point in the future couldn't do my job, again subject to resolution of licensing issues. I'm aware of at least two U.S. public companies that had a non-U.S. lawyer who ran their legal department, although they couldn't call themselves the general counsel because of licensing requirements.

There are already tensions in the U.S. legal system on that front. For example, many U.S. in-house attorneys advise their clients on matters affected by the laws of many of the fifty states in the U.S. I'm not licensed in all fifty states, but as the general counsel I do make final decisions on matters outside of the states I am licensed in. So being a lawyer licensed in one state does not generally prevent the attorney from working for a corporation with operations in other states. One can expand that logic to other countries. I make decisions on matters affected by European Union laws or those of a number of different countries. Of course, I rely upon non-U.S. attorneys to advise me on those local laws, but this is no different than someone advising me on California law before making a decision. By the same logic, couldn't a foreign lawyer in my position do the same with respect to U.S. laws?

If you look at my company, you'll see international diversity all over this U.S.-based company at the executive level: a Brit runs the worldwide Indirect Sales business unit; an Irish runs the Global Services business unit; and a French runs research worldwide. You can get stuck on the U.S. way of looking at things, but if half of your business is done outside the U.S., you have to ask whether only U.S. staff can do the work of your company.

The legal industry is not immune to globalization. I'm a
foreign-born individual who was raised and naturalized
in the U.S. I was born in Korea and came here at the age
of ten. I have a fairly international perspective on many
things. I learned to speak English as a teenager. I believe
in learning something new every day, and learning is
something one should have to do every day. The general
counsel of any multinational company who is licensed in
one country will simply need to learn the laws of other
countries affecting such company.

**Has the economic crisis of 2008 changed your
perspective in any way?**

I have learned to appreciate two things. First, how quickly
the financial markets can fall apart, resulting from the
domino effect of one or two apparently discrete financial
instruments. I recognize that certain key industries or
markets have been identified as causes for the economic
problems, such as the real-estate industry and certain
debt markets. However, I have learned to appreciate
more how interconnected all of these markets are. This
requires us all to be knowledgeable about industries and
markets that we are not directly involved in.

Second, I have learned to appreciate the international
nature of the financial markets. Many Americans don't
realize it, but many outside the U.S. now question the
global financial dominance of the U.S. This economic
crisis started on Wall Street, and more American than
foreign financial-services companies have so far been
burnt by the crisis. At the same time, London and other
financial centers have emerged to prominence. No
country has been immune to the economic downturn
that started in the U.S., and virtually all large companies

have had their financial performance impacted by foreign markets.

Sometimes, I fear the practice of law tends to be so parochial in its nature (with our focus on such things as state license requirements, which were originally designed to keep lawyers in one state from entering into the business of another state) that it's very difficult for lawyers to see outside of those boundaries. This economic crisis is forcing us to look beyond our normal boundaries.

How do you see the role of corporate counsel changing in the next decade?
It's not easy for many lawyers to transition from a law firm to in-house because of the need to assume business responsibilities when in-house. There has been an evolution in the in-house-counsel position, as more attorneys coming in-house have become comfortable with business responsibilities.

There is an increasing need for the general counsel to handle two roles that are not taught at law school. One is a purely managerial role in which you're overseeing legal staff and the business of running a department. From that perspective, it's no different than the managerial roles at other corporate departments. The second is the role in which you're making judgment calls about how best to use legal resources for your client company. Depending on the company, the in-house lawyer is often asked to make those decisions, in contrast to firm lawyers who generally are not asked to make those decisions on their own. General counsel are increasingly making these business decisions on their own.

I think we'll see this trend continue over the next decade. I was advising a friend, who is a litigator, when he was interviewing for a senior in-house legal position at a large company. I told him what the company was looking for was not a lawyer who could advise his business clients, but a businessman who happened to be a litigator.

Three

The Unbundling Trend

New ways to organize legal services

Tasks will become unbundled as a result of business pressures and globalization. The trend of unbundling will climb from lower value tasks up to higher value tasks, and the benefits will be as available to the local niche firm as they will be to the global giant.

The demands of business are pressuring law firms to cut costs, and unbundling tasks is one way to do that. Globalization presents additional pressures on firms to unbundle legal tasks and outsource these tasks to various providers inside and outside the country.

Unbundling separates the attorney's work into discrete tasks, often susceptible to standardization. Law firms and companies can improve efficiency and productivity by unbundling certain tasks and reassigning them. These tasks may be assigned to more appropriate internal employees or contract lawyers rather than associates or junior partners. This is one way to bring pricing more in line with value. Low-level tasks that can be standardized can be priced not according to the premium of the attorney's billable hour but according to the value of the particular task. Law firms employ the unbundling of tasks as one method for meeting the cost-cutting demands of their clients (namely, general counsel, who are themselves under pressure to reduce costs in their corporate legal departments).

When tasks are unbundled and standardized, they may be reassigned to regional providers or, thanks to the fiber-optic cables stretching across the globe, outsourced to providers around the world, such as in Israel, Australia, and India.

What is significant about the unbundling trend is that the tasks are moving up the value chain. Tasks susceptible to unbundling will not only be those typically done by law clerks and paralegals. They will be tasks that lawyers would otherwise bill under a premium hourly rate, such as research, document review, and patent-application review. They will be tasks done by associates and even partners.

"Legal outsourcing in general operates at the low end of the value chain," says Rahul Matthan of Trilegal, an Indian law firm. "As in all cost-arbitrage business models, the greatest risk is from competitors who offer cheaper services. As soon as an entrepreneur proves a business model, dozens of copycats will try to get on the bandwagon by slashing prices. The only sensible strategy in these cases is to have the ability to climb up the value chain and constantly improve the quality of the service offering."

Unbundling will also enable wider collaboration. A project will be organized into tasks. These tasks will be assigned to those best fitted to get them done. A team will be put together. The team will work together to complete the project, and when the project is done, the team will disband. In this way, a team may be composed of a few lawyers from one firm, contract staff from a local provider, and clerks and paralegals on the other side of the world. Tasks will be assigned based on efficiency, experience, and expertise. Team managers will coordinate the project and staff the team. Unbundling will enable a completely new and flexible method for organizing and providing legal services.

Consider movie production. To make a movie, producers pull people together for a specific project. These people combine their skill sets for a limited time, sometimes as short as a day for a single shoot or as long as years for the production of an entire documentary. When the project is completed, people are paid, they disband, and each person moves on to the next project.

This way of working is not new. It is used in many fields and industries. It is just new to legal services. In the legal industry, even companies that are not global firms will now have the technological means to assemble people from all over the world into teams for specific projects. They can pick up the phone and connect with local mediators, international vendors, and legal professionals in various time zones. They can send PDF documents by email or FTP, and ship boxes overnight using UPS or FedEx. They can try to do this on their own, or they can pay consultants or intermediary vendors to help them staff their teams project by project, as needed.

Entrepreneurs in this industry are depending on the unbundling dynamic to drive increasing collaboration and, therefore, the creation of new legal-service models. The new premium compensation will be paid to project managers ("movie producers") who can deliver the desired outcome with increased efficiency and decreased cost.

Entrepreneurs will be taking advantage of these opportunities, but so will law departments, law firms, and other providers. They will be looking to software technology, intranets, and the internet to share information, to access work product, and to foster collaboration among lawyers, staff members and clients.

Think of Google Docs-style document sharing and wiki technology brought into the firm and law department, which is already happening. Lawyers can collaborate, build a storehouse of information for the entire provider, and stockpile documents, templates, agreements, memoranda and other work product on secure servers for any current or future lawyer or staff person to access from any office anywhere. Used in this way, technology can improve efficiency, but it can also strengthen the provider's intrinsic value. Individuals will be supported by the cumulative expertise and collaborative power of the organization. Lawyers will not have to walk the halls and poke their heads into offices, dig through archives, flip through files, scour the books in the library, make repeated calls to other partners or experts, or even search the wider internet. Instead, they will have the history of the provider's work product at their fingertips. They will be able to access it, contribute to it, and leverage it. One lawyer's achievements will be saved and built upon. One team's success will be preserved and refined and made available to everyone.

In the short term, collaborative technology will improve efficiency. In the long term, it will drive quality. It might even come to represent the unique value of the provider itself. Individual lawyers will be able to operate more independently, because they will have the full strength of the provider behind them.

Providers, clients, and consumers are taking greater advantage of the unbundling trend by using information technology, which is explored in more detail in "The Self-help Trend."

"What we've done is to say forget about law or business. Just break the work down to its essence and look at the whole organization."

DAN REED, *CEO*
UNITEDLEX
ATLANTA, GA

INTERVIEW..

What does UnitedLex do?

We provide services that decrease operating costs and improve performance for law firms and corporate legal departments.

How?

By improving process, using technology, and optimizing workflow. This means we do things differently. Business process and technology are the enablers, the drivers toward efficiency and effectiveness. Can we do things faster, at lower cost, and can we do things better?

Does this mean going offshore?

You can send very simple functions offshore, but many things don't go well offshore. With all the talk of the world being flat, for many reasons it's not. It comes down to time zones, skill sets, and other factors. As you move up the skill set toward needing more judgment and knowledge, you can't find that offshore just yet. Maybe in five years. The more complex a task is, and the lower the volume, the less logical it is to move that work offshore. There's a comfort factor and an ease-of-doing-business factor, and the question is how much are those worth? You always need to determine if the change is worth it at that particular time. You don't change for the sake of changing. You only change when it makes sense. The real value is not just in reducing cost. There are issues of quality, timing, location, volume, and control.

What's an example?

Take document review. You can argue that by moving document review offshore, you'll reduce costs, reduce turnaround time, and reduce your error rate. Quality goes up because you're spending more time on your practice, while low-level tasks are being done by people who are totally focused on that low-level task. It's an effort to optimize where the work goes. Most legal work will remain onshore. Using offshore or low-cost can help in certain areas, but the bulk of that will remain where it is.

What did you do before founding UnitedLex?

I was chief financial officer and general counsel to Adjoined Consulting, managing director of Kanbay, and vice president of corporate development and legal affairs at SmartDisk. I also used to work at Ernst & Young and Greenberg Traurig.

How did UnitedLex start?

When I looked at the market a few years ago, I didn't want to start something from scratch. I thought I would buy an existing company or acquire a market leader. The problem was that I found no one who was really doing it.

There were body shops then, operations based purely on labor arbitrage, that is, moving menial tasks to cheaper offshore labor. I wanted to take a consultative approach. So we built ourselves in the model of Accenture.

Other companies, like several of the large offshore outsourcers, view it as labor arbitrage, going for the lowest labor cost. But we don't view it that way. Cost is important, but we have to look at the bigger picture. Does it make sense today, a year from now, two years from now? We need to back it up. Our workers are engineers and consultants, and they approach each assignment from the point of view of leveraging technology and process to optimize the operations of the firm or department within the larger market.

Other companies in this industry get into trouble quickly when they treat legal work like anything else you outsource. They just hire Indian attorneys and let them go. That's not going to work over time. We've always taken a broader, strategic approach, and in a relatively short period, we're the biggest now in this area. We satisfy not just an immediate need but a long-term need.

How does UnitedLex help their clients? What do you do when you walk in the door, and how do you decide what changes need to be made?
Most of our client companies are global. They are *Fortune* 500 or even global 500, and they bring in $10 to $15 billion in annual revenue. We'll come in and look at how contracting is being done. We do an as-is analysis. We map out all their processes. We say, "Forget about going offshore now. What can be done to improve workflow today?" Are papers flowing unnecessarily from Los Angeles to New York to Chicago? Are people redundant,

underskilled, overskilled? Can we use technology and software to increase efficiency? Is there a way to centralize? Can we move part of the process engineering to somewhere in Florida or Austin to lower costs? And only once you've done all that can you ask whether or not it's possible for some type of work to be done in India, China, or Malaysia.

Whatever the function, from litigation to contracts, we try to take out costs at each step of the way. We look at the whole workflow. If a hundred people touch a document, we reduce that to seventy-five. Then, with better use of technology, we might get that number down to forty-five. If we centralize or use offshore resources, we might reduce that even more.

Say you've got ten million documents to review in sixty days. You have many decisions to make very quickly. What part of that work can be performed in Kansas City instead of New York City? Can some be done in India? You want to be able to make those judgments in minutes.

Right now we're doing a project for a $100 billion company. The decisions are taking two months to go through this kind of workflow analysis. We want to get to a point where even more complex projects can be coordinated quickly. Many of our competitors in India adopted a law-firm model. What we've done is to say forget about law or business. Just break the work down to its essence and look at the whole organization.

On the UnitedLex website, there is a section called "The Legal Ecosystem." What is that?
The legal ecosystem refers to the multiple components of the effective and efficient delivery of legal services.

There are strong roles for traditional law firms, whether in the U.S. or global, for in-house resources critical to dealing with various constituencies, and for hybrid vendors like UnitedLex that focus on optimizing critical components to make the entire process far more efficient and effective.

How do you see law firms changing in the next few years?
Law firms play critical roles in the delivery of legal services. The question is just where is it really worth paying $300 to $500 an hour, and where is it worth paying only $25 an hour? The biggest driver of all this change is that top lawyers are costing way too much money. So corporate clients are putting the pressure on. At my former firm, Greenberg Traurig, they're saying it's not an *if* question; it's a *when* question. Corporations lead, and firms follow. It's inevitable. People are now seeing it's not going to be an easy, gradual change. It's going to be violent and very quick. I see it happening now, as more firms try out new tactics to see what works and what doesn't. More and more, they'll be pressured enormously to keep doing that and build on past improvements. But you can't wait too long to start, or you're out of the game.

Four

The Consolidation Trend

New pressure to consolidate providers

Top-tier legal-service providers will continue to consolidate. This consolidation trend is the result of the new global scale of conducting business. Some players in this market will simply not adapt to the new models. They might not be able to afford the investment. They might not be flexible enough to change. They might refuse to change.

In 2000, during the last economic recession, law firms that felt vulnerable consolidated. In 2001, there were 82 mergers in the U.S. Mergers slowed for a few years, then picked up again. According to the consulting firm Hildebrandt, there were 49 mergers in 2004, 52 in 2005, 59 in 2006, 54 in 2007, and 55 in 2008.

Today, we have to acknowledge the uncertainty of the legal industry as the economic crisis of 2008 drags on into 2009 and beyond. Profits are down. Billable hours in many practice areas have dropped significantly. Pay rates are being frozen or reduced. Firms are laying off lawyers and staff. Casualties of the recession include San Francisco's Heller Ehrman, which closed after 118 years, and New York's Thacher Proffitt & Wood, which closed after 160 years.

Consolidation will continue as a survival strategy for many top firms. K&L Gates, for example, merged with three law firms in 2008 and 2009: with Hughes & Luce, a 150-lawyer Dallas firm; with Kennedy Covington, a 175-lawyer Charlotte firm; and most recently with Bell Boyd & Lloyd, a 250-lawyer Chicago firm. K&L Gates expanded to around 1,900 lawyers in thirty-one offices around the world, from Pittsburgh to Taipei. (For updates on mergers, see Altman Weil's merger tracker at www.altmanweil.com.)

The trend toward consolidation among the biggest firms will be driven by the globalization of their client companies and by the desire to do something to protect themselves. Seven U.S. firms merged with overseas firms in 2007, and eight did in 2008. The two largest of 2008 were Mayer Brown's merger with Johnson Stokes & Master of Hong Kong, and Reed Smith's merger with Richards Butler of Hong Kong.

As the trend continues, it is conceivable that only twenty to thirty global legal-service providers will reap the rewards of delivering premium-priced work. These providers will staff 5,000 or more legal professionals. To maintain a global infrastructure, firms will consolidate to serve global companies. They will be able to charge a premium because there will be fewer of them to deliver the required services.

Only those law firms that manage their mergers wisely will overcome the many problems associated with bringing two or more firms under one roof. More levels of management add cost. More lawyers add cost. And two firm cultures create the potential for conflict in many areas, which can aggravate clients. A consolidation combines firm names, brand identities, marketing strategies, rate structures, skill levels, practice areas, client-relationship styles, and management histories. The merger may successfully expand coverage in a target legal area or market, but the combined firm may end up with an odd amalgam of other practice areas, creating an incoherence that might confuse clients who are trying to figure out what it is that the consolidated firm does.

All of this will need to be resolved to optimize the value of the merger and minimize the headaches for the clients. To resolve these issues, the combined leadership will immediately confront the question of how the firm should now be run. The bigger the merger, the more untenable the partnership model becomes. The merged firm will have to transform into a more clearly defined corporate model in order to maintain a strong, coherent structure.

The next tier of firms will be unable to afford a global infrastructure. They will need to pick a geography, industry or practice area in order to justify at least some premium-priced work. By specializing in certain strategic ways, they will be able to put together a profitable model.

One consequence of the consolidation going on at the top tier is that middle firms can pick up those partners or staff who are the casualties of those mergers. By selecting for certain talent, middle firms can specialize in more stable areas, as well as devise strategies for balancing practice areas to accommodate demands for legal services during both good and bad economic times. (According to NALP, as of February 2009, the economic crisis has drained the work in real estate, structured finance, securitization, and mergers and acquisitions, while boosting work in banking, litigation, and regulation.) Middle firms can also select talent moving laterally as well as those lost to mergers. Over 2,500 partners moved from one large law firm to another during the year ending September 30, 2008. At 4% higher than last year, the number sets a new record, according to the *American Lawyer*'s annual survey. The numbers include those forced to leave, those who moved due to mergers, and those lawyers motivated by money or more firm stability. Half the moves were made by lawyers working in corporate law, intellectual property, litigation, and banking and finance. In-house lawyers are also at risk during corporate mergers. As just one recent example, several general counsel and senior in-house lawyers left or were let go from Merrill Lynch in the merger with Bank of America in 2008.

It should be noted that while large firms of a hundred or more attorneys have been getting even larger over the last thirty years, the vast majority of

PRIVATE PRACTITIONERS
BY FIRM SIZE

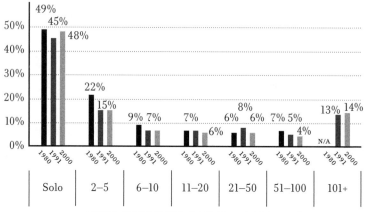

FIRM SIZE BY NUMBER OF ATTORNEYS

The graph shows the percentages of U.S. private practitioners who work in firms of various sizes, including as solo practitioners. Source: *The Lawyer Statistical Report,* American Bar Foundation, 1985, 1994, 2004 editions. Largest firm size for 1980 was 51+ lawyers.

private practitioners work in very small practices of one to five lawyers. According to *The Lawyer Statistical Reports* from the American Bar Foundation, the percentage of medium-sized firms of six to a hundred lawyers has been shrinking, but solo attorneys and firms with two to five lawyers have consistently, since 1980, accounted for two-thirds of all private practitioners. (For more on demographics, see "The People Trend.") This means that most of the 1,162,124 licensed lawyers in the U.S., as of 2008, will not be responding to the recession and the effects of globalization by merging and consolidating. So if they do not go global, they will have to go niche.

Individual lawyers will increasingly subspecialize in many areas, performing work such as software licensing, internet law, security compliance, and military law. Niche work is one way lawyers respond to the marketplace as new areas of growth open up to business. Lawyers have always specialized, but as technologies grow more complex, businesses more global, and markets more fragmented, some lawyers will narrow their fields of expertise to a nearly laser-like focus. An attorney may become like a surgeon who specializes in a single, highly complex operation.

Firms may specialize by catering to a narrow market segment defined by geography, industry, or legal service. As a business strategy, specialization can improve the firm's focus, the quality of service, and its use of resources. It can strengthen its reputation and provide the rationale for investing in technology and other process improvements that would increase the value of their services and, by extension, inspire client referrals.

By focusing on niche markets, firms may also improve their business models in direct response to their clients' needs. Niche firms can more easily scrap the billable hour and experiment with more flexible pricing and more creative use of legal staff and resources, including computer and communications technology. Niche firms can also more directly engage in client partnering, namely by seeking feedback, using performance metrics, and making continuous improvements.

Firms that do not merge or specialize can compete for commodity work. The definition of commodity legal work varies, but in essence it refers to work that is routine, simple, lower value, relatively frequent, and subject to a common process, if not to outright standardization. It might include routine contracts, standard agreements, document review, and other low-risk transactions the lawyer or firm may do on a daily basis. These common, low-risk tasks demand little legal knowledge, and they may be streamlined according to an improved process or via the use of information technology. These tasks are susceptible to unbundling, standardization and outsourcing to contract staff, local vendors, or international third-party providers.

To compete in the commodity market where the margins are slim, the firm or provider must work continuously to add value to the process through better use of staffing, resources, and technology. They will have to give up premium, hourly-rate pricing. They will have to use global resources to turn a profit. They will not be able to turn a profit on commodity work by remaining local or even national. They may provide legal services to local or regional clients, of course, but to compete, they must develop a business model with a global reach in order to leverage more affordable labor and flexible, streamlined services. The traditional model based on leveraging full-time permanent associates will be replaced by a model leveraging temporary combinations of outsourced labor, contract lawyers, and in-house professionals.

Another strategy should be noted: going public. Around the world, regulations prohibit law firms from being publicly owned and traded corporations. Non-lawyers cannot own law firms. The prohibition is based on the expectation that non-lawyer shareholders would pressure lawyers to put profit first and their clients second. Legal advice would become tainted by economic motives, and clients would question whether the services they were buying were necessary. In other words, the system of incentives created by public ownership of law firms might undermine the sound provision of legal services and the trust in the attorney/client relationship. One country decided to try it anyway. Australia became the first country to change the rules, and in 2007 Slater & Gordon became the world's first publicly traded law firm.

The shares for Slater & Gordon, a 140-lawyer personal-injury firm in Melbourne, sold at twice the firm's book value. The partners doubled their wealth. Creating wealth for the partners, however, cannot justify going public, especially during today's global recession. Share prices can just as easily plummet if partners make poor business decisions, efficiencies are not realized, or major corporate clients go bank-rupt. Instead, the motivations for going public should be strategic and structural. Outside ownership could usher in a more corporate style of management. The traditional structure of the law firm could be disman-tled and reorganized. Innovations in management, organizational structure, information technology, compensation, staffing, and everything else could result in the more efficient delivery of higher quality legal services.

While it is too soon to predict the results of Australia's experiment in publicly owned law firms, the UK has decided to follow suit and has changed British law to allow outside investment in law firms. Nothing can happen until the Legal Services Board, a regulatory body, is established, but the expectation is that UK firms will be able to go public by 2011.

The larger U.S. and Canadian law firms are paying attention, but they should be doing more than that. They should anticipate the competitive advantages that a sudden burst of capital may provide UK law firms. In light of that, they should re-evaluate their current models and plan for yet another inevitable shift in the global legal marketplace.

*"Our largest institutional clients
want the best legal advice and
they want the best service at the
lowest rate.... We must staff
efficiently if we are to make money
as a law firm."*

TYRONE C. FAHNER, *Partner*
MAYER BROWN LLP
CHICAGO, IL

INTERVIEW..

What trend has impacted your firm the most?
The biggest trend in the last several years has been the
necessary growth which has occurred as a result of
globalization. There is no real way to protect your client
base any longer unless you can cover a good part of the
world or have relationships with other firms around the
world. For those firms doing international work, such
as corporate deals or structured finance, the change has
been profound. Any firm that is only capable to advise on
the U.S. portion of a deal risks losing that work. We have
expanded our geographic reach accordingly.

How has the recent crisis affected your work?
In the current economic situation, almost every firm's
workflow is down. We are doing well, considering the
marketplace, because some years ago we extended our
U.S. footprint into Western Europe and two years ago
into China, Thailand, and Vietnam. The U.S. and Europe

have felt the effects of recession, but we are doing well as a firm because of the relative strength of the Asian practice. We are doing restructurings and deals for global companies, and we are using every part of our firm.

How has your law firm evolved over the years?

When I joined Mayer Brown in 1979, we had about 175 lawyers in the U.S., mostly Chicago. About nine years ago, we had grown to about 650 lawyers, and they were still mainly in the U.S. Twenty-eight lawyers were in London. We had been there for thirty years, but few knew it. There was generally a lack of international work, so between 1998 and 2006, we increased our international presence immensely. We grew to 1,550 lawyers. We expanded across the globe. We added 300 lawyers in London and over 200 in Germany, Paris and Brussels. In 2008, we merged with JSM (Johnson Stokes & Master), a firm in China, Thailand and South Vietnam, and that gave us our Asian presence. We also have an office in Sao Paulo, Brazil. And today we are over 1,800 lawyers.

Can a firm get into trouble overextending itself in that direction?

You can easily fail if you overrepresent your ability and scope as a firm. Especially in a global economy, you will lose a client and never win them back. You must be careful not to oversell your services. It is important to know your client's business.

How have your relationships with your corporate clients changed?

Our largest institutional clients want the best legal advice and they want the best service at the lowest rate. Six years ago, requests for proposals were rare. Now they are an everyday occurrence. We must staff efficiently if we are to make money as a law firm.

Certain general counsel insist on the best lawyers no matter what the cost, and others will tell you they are going through a difficult financial time and want to negotiate a cap for a given project or assignment. From automotive to pharmaceuticals to energy, companies are in difficult times. We do not believe in take-it-or-leave-it pricing. If you are inflexible, clients leave you, no matter what your historical relationship.

Do you use temporary staffing or outsourcing?
We have outsourced document review to India in the past, and we are involved in several matters that are highly labor intensive. We have our lawyers supervising the operation, but we have hired contract lawyers because we can hire them more affordably. You must be creative.

In your experience, how have general counsel been reacting to increasing pressure to reduce costs?
The reality is that lawyers outside of the company are an expense item. The same thing is true for law departments. If general counsel cannot control costs in proportion to the company's legal issues, they won't be there long. For years certain firms have been able to charge whatever they wanted, and general counsel would pay so as to cover themselves; if things went south, they could say that at least they hired the best (i.e., most expensive) lawyers. There is still some of that going on, but mostly that dynamic has changed.

What trends in law firms have you seen over the years?
Support staff has been shrinking. Older lawyers still have secretaries because we cannot use the computer as effectively as most younger lawyers. So the overhead at firms has come down in terms of support staff, because young lawyers can do it all on their computers. Our firm uses fewer paralegals and secretaries now because of

this trend, even though we have increased the number of our lawyers. The dynamic of law practice has changed dramatically.

Another trend is technology. We spend a tremendous amount of money on IT and communications systems, because if you cannot communicate with your clients on their systems, you are out of luck. A firm our size can spend around $30 or $40 million a year just to stay up to date, and that is just for basic technology. We do all the support work in-house, but it is one of our largest expenses. Our technology department and support group are over 200 people. We do it so we can control things within our system. We spend more than most, but we have found it to be essential to our success.

Five
The Self-help Trend
New ways to know about legal services

Consumers and clients know more about the law than ever before. Information is more available, and the industry is more transparent.

This is not only true in the law. It is a social trend. We have greater access to information. There are more books written about the law than ever before, and we can conduct our own research online, from home. Computer and communications technology enable us and empower us. We can use the internet, Lexis/Nexis, Westlaw, and myriad search engines to demystify the legal profession and its expertise and arcana. When barriers between people and information are removed, the mystique of law dissipates.

There are now more than 1 billion internet users around the world, according to comScore (China has the most, with the U.S. in second), and as the number of users increases, so does the size and content of the internet. As an example, Google continues its mission to scan all books into its searchable online database. Type in "legal self-help" in Google Book Search, and the search returns 5,820 titles (and is sure to grow). Here is a short list of websites that offer legal information, search functions, advice, forums, referrals, links, and other resources:

AllLaw.com

CataLaw.com

FindForms.com

FindLaw.com

FreeAdvice.com

FreeLegalForms.net

GotTrouble.com

Internet Legal Research Group
(ilrg.com)

JurisDictionary.com

LawCheck.com

LawGuru.com

LawInfo.com

LawSource.com

'Lectric Law Library
(lectlaw.com)

LegalDocs.com

Legal Services Resource
Corporation
(lri.lsc.gov)

Martindale.com

USLegalForms.com

WaterlowLegal.com

WorldLawDirect.com

There are, of course, many, many more.

Traditionally, professions like law, medicine and even accounting guarded their castles of expertise behind walls of jargon and moats of insider knowledge. Lawyers knew the rules, and they knew the rule-makers. Outsiders could not gain access. Outsiders had to hire their own attorneys. And they had to do this without knowing how to judge the relative merits of different attorneys, except by reputation. Once hired, the lawyers did not part with their expertise or their knowledge. They used their knowledge on behalf of the client, who was happy to walk away confused as long as he could walk away.

Today? Today, information is both king and currency. And while it takes time to track down the information, and effort to figure out what to do with it, people are increasingly willing to do so. They are willing to share their information, their experience, and their opinions. (In a 2007 survey, comScore found that nearly 80% of online users who shopped for legal services relied on online reviews to make their choices, citing consumer reviews as more influential than professional reviews.) In one way, you can look at what Amazon is doing to big-box retailers, what YouTube is doing to mainstream network and cable television, and even what Wikipedia is doing to traditional encyclopedias and libraries, and find precedents for what the rise of legal information technology can do to the mainstream legal industry and traditional law firms. A whole lot of people empowered by easy access to the internet opens a new kind of marketplace, one in which anyone can compete and in which competition is fierce.

Mediators are increasingly willing to filter this information, present it concisely, and disseminate it widely. H&R Block offers software for wills, trusts and estate planning. Nolo Press has been selling legal self-help books and documents since 1971, and its online presence, Nolo.com, continues to expand its online resources. LegalZoom.com not only offers forms and documents but, for a fee, prepares them and files them. They offer services in several areas, including wills and trusts, business formation, divorce, intellectual property, small claims, bankruptcy, and real estate.

It is often risky to be your own lawyer. While any adult eighteen or older can draw up a will, trust, or other estate-planning document without a lawyer, state regulations vary widely when it comes to witness and notary requirements, and the bigger the estate or the more complicated the situation, the greater reason a person has to consult a lawyer. It is likely that many people buy the documents, learn a bit on their own, realize the difficulties involved, and then ultimately decide to consult a lawyer. Still, self-help legal kits and other resources provide an introduction to an otherwise mysterious practice. Self-help resources provide a means of comparison and a frame of reference. (Consider how much more today's patients know—or think they know—from websites like WebMD about prescription drugs, diagnoses, and prognoses when they meet with their family physicians.) When consumers have learned a certain amount on their own, they can better judge how well their lawyers are serving them and what value they are receiving. They can tell when lawyers are just filling in the blanks in a standard template.

When individuals choose to represent themselves in court rather than hire attorneys, these *pro se* litigants cannot only avail themselves of online information and self-help kits; they can also find support from *pro se* assistance programs sponsored by courts, bar associations, and even law schools.

They can purchase unbundled tasks or services from lawyers without hiring these lawyers to take on their entire matters or cases. A lawyer can provide the *pro se* litigant with unbundled services such as advice, research, discovery assistance, negotiation assistance, and document drafting. The lawyer can be a legal coach or assistant coach; the lawyer can even participate in certain court appearances. The self-help and unbundling trends dovetail in this area and reinforce each other. While some members of the legal community worry about the fairness, efficiency and even ethics involved in self-representation boosted by unbundling, the benefits include an improvement of the quality of *pro se* representation, an expansion of access to legal support and expertise, and a greater opportunity for individuals to obtain justice. It is possible that in the near future we will see the empowerment of *pro se* litigants combine with enhanced technology in order to improve the efficiency and fairness of entire court systems.

Representing corporate and business clients, general counsel are becoming more knowledgeable about costs the more that legal tasks are unbundled, subject to competitive pricing, and sent out to third-party vendors, entrepreneurs, and even contract staff. The internet and computer technology enable the dissemination of information and work, and this pressures law firms to follow in the footsteps of other businesses that have taken advantage of moving work electronically (using databases, software and networking) to the people who can perform the work at a price in proportion to its value.

Thanks to technology and information, general counsel (and the public) are learning more about industry practices and the inner workings of law firms. Legal surveys are generated constantly (and disseminated widely and instantly) by a variety of companies, such as Altman Weil, Forrester Research, Hildebrandt, ValueNotes, Deloitte Touche Tohmatsu, Citi Private Bank, Incisive Legal Intelligence, and PriceWaterhouseCoopers, as well as by industry associations, such as the American Bar Association, NALP (Association for Legal Career Professionals), and the Association of Corporate Counsel (ACC). And lists, rankings, surveys, and scorecards are generated daily by print and online media, such as *American Lawyer, The National Law Journal*, the *ABA Journal*, and the *Wall Street Journal*. The explosion of blogging has happened in the legal industry, as it has in every industry, with professional blogs from *The National Law Journal* and *American Lawyer* to amateur sites like AbovetheLaw.com and LawShucks.com, the latter species providing gossip, opinion, insider information, and even breaking news and statistics. Thanks to the internet, legal journalism can be practiced by anyone with free time and a computer.

Inevitably, more entrepreneurs will recognize opportunities. They will develop new ways to build databases of searchable information and provide new ways to access legal services. JDSupra.com, for example, allows legal professionals (from lawyers and firms to public-interest groups and law professors) to create profiles and upload documents, articles, and examples of their legal work. More importantly, it allows users free access to search this information, including lawyer and law-firm profiles, court filings, decisions, forms, articles, alerts, and newsletters. Founded by former litigator Aviva Cuyler, JD Supra is intended to be used by legal professionals to showcase their work, by consumers to conduct legal research and search for lawyers, and by the media to learn of new cases (in the "Hot Docs" section) and find experts on newsworthy legal topics. Entrepreneurs in this area will continue to break barriers to information, enable better ways to search larger databases, increase collaboration through online networks, and design new systems that reward users and create value for all who participate.

I do not know exactly what tomorrow's model will look like. I do not know exactly how far information technology will boost providers toward global collaboration, lawyers toward empowered independence, or consumers toward self-sufficiency. I do know that educated clients are already putting more pressure on the legal profession. They are demanding alternatives to the billable hour. They are demanding more variety and more nuance in pricing and service. They are assigning new values to tasks based on complexity. Emboldened by information, clients are not just shopping for better deals; they are looking for better ways to shop. Empowered by technology, legal providers cannot just cut prices for their services; they have to find new ways to work.

"My goals are to present data in a useful fashion and to provide insider commentary on relevant stories."

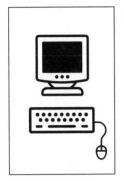

ANONYMOUS*, *Editor*
LAWSHUCKS.COM

INTERVIEW...

What's your motivation for running the site in general?
I wanted to do something entrepreneurial. In-house
counsel at a financial-services company wasn't
scratching that itch. I felt like there was a substantial
niche not being served by any of the legal blogs or
newspapers. I've been practicing for ten years, and the
existing options were either aimed at (or overrun by) law
students or very junior associates, or were completely
professional. Practicing attorneys still gossip—in fact,
maybe more so than junior lawyers or law students.
We know lots more people and have a common base of
information.

**What's your motivation in compiling layoff figures in
particular?**
I didn't expect it to take off like it has. I wanted a single
point of reference that presented the data in the way
that allows them to be used for analysis. As is typical

---

* The editor revealed his identity but requested anonymity, which is
maintained on LawShucks.com.

for lawyers, numbers were being analyzed with, and
presented as, words. That seemed flawed to me,
so I set about creating a solution that was useful. I
assumed others would feel similarly, but because of the
transparency in my methods, I've been surprised by how
widely it's being cited.

**How do you see your role? Do you consider yourself, for
example, a new breed of online industry-insider e-
journalist, or are you just a guy who posts information
important to your peers?**
I don't think it's a particularly new breed, other than in
comparison to traditional print media. There have been
others doing similar things for some time now. David Lat
[editor-in-chief of AbovetheLaw.com, an online legal
tabloid] is the obvious example, but he has clearly gotten
out of the day-to-day writing part of the business. I
certainly don't think a lot of the information I'm posting
is important to my peers, but I try to make the stuff I post
either interesting or informative. The Layoff Tracker is
only one of the components of the site. My goals are to
present data in a useful fashion and to provide insider
commentary on relevant stories. I'd also like to see more
of a community develop on the site—I'm far from the
only lawyer with an opinion—and have a few plans in
mind. I just need to find time to implement them.

**Do you maintain your anonymity, or do your readers
know who you are? Do you still work in a big firm, or
did you change your career and if so why?**
Anonymous. I try to do this nights and weekends but,
as with any new toy, I check on it from time to time
during the day. I don't need a bunch of gossip around
the office about how I'm wasting my time blogging while
the economy is going down the toilet. I spent seven

LAYOFFS OF ATTORNEYS AND STAFF
AMONG BIG LAW FIRMS IN THE U.S.

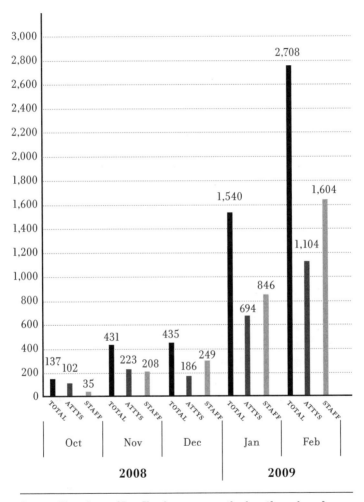

Source: The editor of LawShucks.com compiles layoff numbers from the *Wall Street Journal, American Lawyer,* and other sources. As this book went to press in early March, LawShucks tallied 5,408 layoffs among large law firms for the calendar year 2009. The broader legal industry lost 4,200 net jobs in the month of February 2009, according to the U.S. Labor Department's Bureau of Labor Statistics. In that month, nationwide unemployment rose from 7.6% to 8.1%.

years at a big firm in New York City doing mergers and acquisitions, then went in-house when my wife was pregnant with our first child. I'm currently at a *Fortune* 100 financial-services company, so it's not the greatest environment right now.

You compile numbers that over time track certain trends. What are the most important trends that you see at work?

It's really just a continuation of the larger monkey-see, monkey-do trend of Big Law. Some firm does some thing for some reason, a few others follow, then the floodgates are open. This time around, we had Cadwalader starting the layoffs. That emboldened firms like Dechert and Dewey & LeBoeuf. Thelen and Thacher Proffitt also had layoffs, but it was too little, too late in their cases. Actually, the other trend we see is traditional Big Law one-upmanship, albeit in a very unfortunate manner. Firms are being as aggressive as they can while the public perception is tolerant of the practice.

I will say that one practice that is completely despicable is "stealth layoffs." It's abhorrent that firms are changing their standards of review in order to cull their ranks. The sole purpose is some misguided attempt to save face by throwing attorneys under the bus. If I were looking at firms right now, I'd go to the firms with the massive, announced layoffs rather than those engaged in this deceitful behavior.

In five years, where do you see the biggest trends going?

When I was at a previous employer, I asked, "So, how do we make money?" The answer was, "Inertia." Same thing goes for law firms. The billable hour hasn't always been around. It was a response to a need for more transparency into billing. For a much longer time than the billable hour has been around, the practice was for clients to get a bill "for services rendered" and a single amount. That wouldn't work these days. Firms and clients have plenty of data on how long it takes to do certain things. No one has done a good job of aggregating, synthesizing and processing that information. Yes, we like to think all mergers and all lawsuits are unique, but when you have enough data, you see that no particular deal is likely to be different. It really just becomes a risk-allocation issue: is the client going to overpay for the deal that's too easy, or is the firm going to take a haircut on the lawsuit that gets too complicated?

If I were the firms, I'd be pushing like crazy for this, because it's a lot easier for me to compare data across multiple clients and put in a reasonable cushion. Clients typically use one firm for one kind of deal, so they just assume that the firm takes that long to do that kind of work. And if I had my druthers, firms would be eating most of the cost of the first few years' practice anyway. In most situations, I prefer to pay the higher rate for a more senior lawyer than to allow a junior lawyer to take the first crack at anything.

Six

The People Trend

New shifts in the demographics of legal professionals

People trends are complex. Data samples vary. Categories may overlap. Definitions may be rough. A trend measured over years may be insignificant when compared to the trend measured over decades. Numbers give at best a snapshot of what you are trying to observe.

But it is always worth exploring demographic trends. They can point to new insights and new opportunities. The types of people working in the legal industry have changed, and so have their attitudes. There is more diversity today: in age, gender, race, and nationality, as well as in people's attitudes about work, lifestyles and technology. And the increasing diversity of people and their attitudes cannot help but change the way things are done.

One of the most significant shifts in the demographics of the legal industry has been the rise of women. The following numbers are based on enrollment statistics for ABA-accredited law schools. In the 1963–64 school year, 3.7% of the students enrolled in J.D. programs were women. Ten years later, 16% were women. Twenty years later, 38.3% were women. Thirty years later, 43.1% were women. And by the 2003–04 school year, 48.7% were women. Women made it to

ENROLLMENT IN ABA LAW SCHOOLS

ACADEMIC YEAR	NUMBER OF SCHOOLS	TOTAL JD ENROLLMENT	MALE JD ENROLLMENT	FEMALE JD ENROLLMENT	% FEMALE ENROLLMENT
2007–08	198	141,719	75,523	66,196	46.7%
2006–07	195	141,031	74,946	66,085	46.8%
2005–06	191	140,298	73,685	66,613	47.5%
2004–05	188	140,376	72,938	67,438	48.0%
2003–04	187	137,676	70,649	67,027	48.7%
2002–03	186	132,885	67,706	65,179	49.0%
2001–02	184	127,610	65,134	62,476	49.0%
2000–01	183	125,173	64,540	60,633	48.4%
1999–00	182	125,184	65,822	59,362	47.4%
1998–99	181	125,627	67,675	57,952	46.1%
1997–98	178	125,886	68,971	56,915	45.2%
1996–97	179	128,623	71,500	57,123	44.4%
1995–96	178	129,397	72,436	56,961	44.0%
1994–95	177	128,989	73,181	55,808	43.2%
1993–94	176	127,802	72,668	55,134	43.1%
1992–93	166	128,212	63,568	64,644	50.4%
1991–92	176	129,580	74,470	55,110	42.5%
1990–91	175	127,261	73,164	54,097	42.5%
1989–90	175	124,471	71,358	53,113	42.7%
1988–89	174	120,694	69,762	50,932	42.2%
1987–88	175	117,997	69,077	48,920	41.5%
1986–87	175	117,813	69,893	47,920	40.7%
1985–86	175	118,700	71,214	47,486	40.0%
1984–85	174	119,847	72,950	46,897	39.1%
1983–84	173	121,201	74,840	46,361	38.3%
1982–83	172	121,791	76,252	45,539	37.4%
1981–82	172	120,879	77,634	43,245	35.8%
1980–81	171	119,501	78,667	40,834	34.2%

Source: ABA Law School Enrollment statistics, 1963–2008

50% only once, when they were 50.4% of the 1992–93 law-school population. Since 1986, however, the percentage of women in law schools has remained solidly in the 40% to 50% range. The percentage rose to 49% for two school years in a row, from 2001–03, perhaps as a result of the downturn in the economy after 2000. Remarkably, however, it has not dipped below 45% since the 1996–97 school year, when it was 44.4%.

The trend is significant for many reasons. It only took women twenty-two years to go from less than 4% to over 40% of the law-school population. And once they achieved that, they stayed there. Despite the difficulty of balancing private lives with private practice (and of parenting tracks with partnership tracks), women have never left the law in droves. Their percentage has varied in the last thirty years, but looked at over decades, the numbers confirm the permanence of the achievement.

The presence of more women in the law (in law schools and in law jobs) has changed the types of courses taught, the kind of law practiced, and the way law is practiced. Hundreds of authors have already written extensively on these changes. For my limited purposes in this book, I want only to identify the general trend and to explore women's specific impact on employment relationships.

PROFESSIONAL WOMEN AT WORK

Women made up **30%** of the legal profession in 2007.

Women made up **18%** of partners,

44% of associates, and

47% of summer associates in 2005.

Women made up **16%** of *Fortune* 1000 general counsel in 2006.

Sources, top to bottom: American Bar Association Marketing Research Department 2007; NALP, 2005; MCCA 2006 *Fortune* 1000 General Counsel Survey.

Women have introduced alternatives to full-time employment. Communications and computer technologies have further enabled these alternatives. People can work part-time or flex-time. They can work from home. Women can take maternity leave. The bind of working mothers has not been resolved, however, and working women today are faced with a difficult choice. They have to sacrifice (or at least postpone) their education and their careers in order to have children. Women are therefore much more likely than men to look for flexible careers. The law firm of the future needs to provide this flexibility. This flexibility is more easily achieved in transactional, project-related work than in litigation or in more time-sensitive work.

According to a 2008 NALP survey, 98% of law firms allow lawyers to work part-time, and 5.6% of attorneys do so, about 74% of whom are women. Last year, 5.4% of attorneys worked part-time and 75% were women. The numbers are slowly increasing. In 1994, only 86% of law firms supported part-time work, and 2.4% of attorneys did so. Currently, 4.9% of associates work part-time, 90% of whom are women; 3.2% of partners work part-time, 70% of whom are women; and 20% of staff attorneys and of counsel work part-time.

Women's breakthroughs in promoting flexible working schedules have paved the way for men and those of the next generations. Men may choose to work flex-time for reasons of lifestyle or parenting. Members of Generation X are more likely than Baby Boomers to be dual-working parents and to work from home, telecommute, or job-share. Generation Xers have different aspirations, but they also grew up with the technology that enables these more flexible working relationships. This is even more so the case with members of Generation Y, who are not only more internet-savvy but more likely to collaborate with others using everything from iPhones and Blackberrys to Facebook and Google Docs.

It is Finally Time for Flex-time and Teamwork

Flexible work is a nexus of many trends. More people are interested in working flex-time or in nontraditional relationships. This includes men and women, Generations X and Y, solo practitioners, contract lawyers, and even senior partners who do not want to retire but do not want to work at the same pace.

Communication and computer technology has enabled people to telecommute and to work with others all over the world. The pressures on the legal industry to dismantle the billable hour, unbundle and standardize tasks, and reassign work to experts who can perform at more reasonable prices are persuading law firms, law departments and other legal-service providers to reorganize their business models. Put all this together, and you can see a new way of working emerging on the horizon. People can use collaborative technologies to work in temporary teams to perform unbundled tasks for specific projects. When that project is done, the team disbands, and everyone moves on to the next project.

And the people who come together on these teams can be, in theory, from anywhere. A team may be composed of a firm partner, a contract attorney, an at-home legal professional, and an overseas professional. It will be up to the provider to match the appropriate business and legal strategies and to organize these collaborative teams quickly and efficiently.

I have already mentioned how this way of working will give rise to new roles for legal professionals as legal architects, legal managers, team leaders, and chief legal officers, from those who put the teams together to those who oversee their operations. The people who fill these new roles may have law degrees, business degrees, or neither. They may work full-time for a provider, a firm, or a staffing company, or they too may work flex-time or freelance. At any rate, in the years to come, this new way of working will provide fertile opportunities for entrepreneurs, providers, and legal professionals.

The pace at which the legal industry is responding to these opportunities has been accelerated by the recent and ongoing economic crisis. In a recent article in the *Legal Intelligencer,* Deborah Epstein Henry, founder of Flex-Time Lawyers (see the interview at the end of this section), suggests that law firms avoid layoffs and instead allow talented lawyers to work flex-time during the down market. Both parties benefit. The lawyer stays employed and experiments with a different work/life balance, while the firm retains its relationship with talented lawyers while saving money through reduced salaries. When the market picks up, the lawyer may return to full-time work, and the law firm is not caught understaffed.

The Three Generations

Generational trends support the larger trend explored above, that of a rising diversity of technology-empowered people collaborating in teams, project by project.

The three most commonly identified generations are the Baby Boomers, Generation X, and Generation Y (or Millennials, so-called for being the first to come of age in the new millennium). Defining their boundaries, however, is problematic. According to the U.S. Census Bureau, Baby Boomers are the 80 million Americans born after World War II between 1946 and 1964. Other estimates put the Boomers at 76 million born from 1946 to 1960. The Boomers are the simplest to categorize, because they are defined with reference to the historical marker of the end of WWII.

Generation X is the trickiest generation to define. Their markers and numbers are all over the map. They have been estimated to be between 41 and 50 million Americans born between 1961–1981, 1964–1974, 1965–1976, 1965–1980, or 1966–1976.

Finding the boundaries for Generation Y depends on where you mark the end of Generation X, but the end point for Y is easier, generally taken to be around the turn of the millennium. The members of Generation Y have been estimated to be between 70 and 78 million Americans born between 1976–2001, 1977–1994, 1977–2002, 1978–1989, 1978–2000, or 1982–2001. The current Yers in the workforce (18- to 28-year olds) number around 38 million U.S. citizens.

If the Boomers are those born between 1946 and 1964, Generation X can be considered to be the generation born during the next eighteen years, from 1965 to 1983, which makes Generation Y those born from 1984 to 2002. However, generations measured in increments of eighteen years do not match the cultural definitions of these generations, which are based on combinations of factors, such as cultural milestones, technological advances, and major historical events (which is why some commentators are pinpointing Generation Z to be those born either after the turn of the millennium or else after September 11, 2001).

But measuring these generations in terms other than years may explain some of the differences in

ESTIMATED POPULATIONS OF THE GENERATIONS

Sources: U.S. Census Bureau; "Gen-X: The Ignored Generation?" by M.J. Stephey in *Time Magazine*, April 16, 2008; "Generation Y: They've Arrived at Work with a New Attitude," by Stephanie Armour in *USA Today*, November 8, 2005; and *X Saves the World*, by Jeff Gordinier (2008).

population tallies. If you use the cultural definitions of the generations, you would identify the Boomers as those born during a period of eighteen years from 1946 to 1964; the Gen Xers, during a period of eleven years from 1965 to 1976; and the Gen Yers or Millennials, during a period of twenty-three years from 1977 to 2000. Measured this way, it is no surprise that there will be more Boomers and Yers and fewer Xers, and that in general is the assumption of most commentators on the subject. Boomers consist of nearly 80 million people, Gen Xers only around 45 million, and Gen Yers back up around 76 million.

For this book, the relevance of marking these generational numbers lies in tracking the working experiences of the generations as they enter and leave the workforce. The Boomers and Generation Y have the advantage of influencing the workplace by virtue of sheer numbers. Generation X has been labeled the transitional generation sandwiched between two larger generations. So the influences of Generation X may be felt more as specific advances, from the insistence on more equitable work/life balances to the establishment of transformative technologies. In one sense, Generation X is the linchpin in the transition from a Boomer economy based on corporate careerism to the coming Generation Y economy based on unbound collaboration.

Ultimately, it is best not to rely too heavily on rigid generational boundaries. In general, Boomers have peaked and are retiring, Gen Xers are maturing in the workplace, and Gen Yers are up and coming. This way, it makes sense to explore the trends in consumption and technology as these affect group attitudes about work and lifestyle.

Last year, Forrester Research published the 2008 North America Technographics Benchmark report, which was based on a mail survey of nearly 61,000 consumers representing 53,000 households in the United States and Canada. The results revealed trends in the uses of technology for work, communication, shopping, and entertainment among the generations.

Overall, as might have been predicted, younger generations rely on technology in greater numbers

POPULATION TRENDS TO 2050

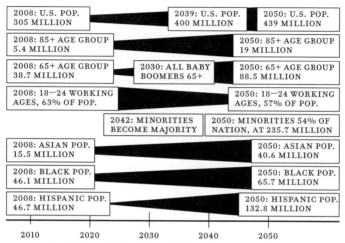

2008: U.S. POP. 305 MILLION	2039: U.S. POP. 400 MILLION	2050: U.S. POP. 439 MILLION
2008: 85+ AGE GROUP 5.4 MILLION		2050: 85+ AGE GROUP 19 MILLION
2008: 65+ AGE GROUP 38.7 MILLION	2030: ALL BABY BOOMERS 65+	2050: 65+ AGE GROUP 88.5 MILLION
2008: 18—24 WORKING AGES, 63% OF POP.		2050: 18—24 WORKING AGES, 57% OF POP.
	2042: MINORITIES BECOME MAJORITY	2050: MINORITIES 54% OF NATION, AT 235.7 MILLION
2008: ASIAN POP. 15.5 MILLION		2050: ASIAN POP. 40.6 MILLION
2008: BLACK POP. 46.1 MILLION		2050: BLACK POP. 65.7 MILLION
2008: HISPANIC POP. 46.7 MILLION		2050: HISPANIC POP. 132.8 MILLION

2010   2020   2030   2040   2050

Sources: "An Older and More Diverse Nation by Midcentury," by Robert Bernstein and Tom Edwards, a news release from the U.S. Census Bureau, August 14, 2008.

and at greater rates, while technology is becoming increasingly wireless, portable and personalized. Today's typical older person has a landline telephone, a desktop computer, and a home theater; he or she shops at the mall, watches television, and works at an office. Today's typical young person has a cellphone, a laptop computer, and an MP3 player; he or she shops online, watches YouTube, and telecommutes.

Here are some of the specific findings of the Benchmark report.

Generations X and Y are ditching their landline telephones in favor of cellphones and internet voice technologies. Only half of Gen Y consumers use landlines, compared with 80% of seniors. Four of five households have a cellphone, while 91% of Gen Y households do. And the mobile devices are used for more than voice. They are used for taking photos and videos, sending text, storing music, playing games, and most importantly accessing the internet.

Eighty-six percent of U.S. homes have a personal computer. More than half of Gen Y consumers have laptops, and they use them for personal and entertainment reasons (photos, music, videos, internet access) at a higher rate than older consumers. Gen Xers prefer TVs and cellphones for household and personal use, while Gen Yers prefer personal devices, like iPhones and iPods, that provide online access to media and social networks.

Three-quarters of North American adults use the internet monthly or more, averaging almost fifteen hours per week. Boomers and Gen Xers are most likely to bank online. Boomers represent 38% of all online shoppers; Gen Xers, 34%. Gen Yers are early adopters of new media technologies and spend more time going online for entertainment and to use social networks than they spend using offline media, like watching TV. More Gen Yers visit YouTube each week than watch MTV.

Twenty-two percent of North American households have a home network. In 2007, the growth rate was 12%, but in 2008 the growth was 20%. Gen Yers and Gen Xers are more likely to have home networks, and they are connecting multiple computers, cell-phones, MP3 players, and game consoles.

Twenty-one percent of North American adults work from home. They run their own businesses, tele-commute, or take home company work. The majority of home workers rely heavily on technology.

The survey results tend to confirm common-sense intuitions about the prevalence of technology and the state of the consumer marketplace. It is easy to see how the generational attitudes toward working are being facilitated and reinforced by advances in technology. As technology becomes more personal, connected, and portable, so do workers become more independent, collaborative, and mobile. These advances are what make possible, if not inevitable, new models for working in the legal industry, from virtual law firms and global legal providers to online lawyer networks and flex-time telecommuters.

The Generations at Work in the Law

Attitude changes do not arise out of thin air. They often arise in reaction to prevailing circumstances. Women entered law schools in greater numbers in the 1960s not because women as a whole suddenly decided to like the law, but because the social movements for civil rights and women's rights compelled law schools to open their doors to women and minorities. And women do not continue to press for flexible schedules because they cannot handle the pace of work, but because women want the choice to have and raise children without sacrificing their entire careers to do so. Generations X and Y are more tech-savvy not because they like personal computers and digital technology more than Baby Boomers, but because they have grown up around them (Generation X from the mid-Eighties, and Generation Y from the cradle).

And today's associates are not more disloyal out of a sudden shift in their emotional outlook, but because today's law firms can no longer promise a steady track to partnership. In response, today's young associates have had to become opportunistic. Young lawyers can no longer afford to be loyal associates toiling away in a basement cubicle for seven years until the rays of partnership shine upon them in saving grace. Young people have adapted, and they are now opportunists, leaving today's firm for tomorrow's promotion, forever fielding calls from recruiters scouting for the next move up the ladder. Having watched these steady changes over the years, as well as witnessed the recession's severe shock to the law-firm model, young people today have to re-evaluate both their reasons for going to law school and their expectations of working as a lawyer.

An intersection of trends is bound to affect law-school enrollment. The school year of 1993–94 was the first time that over 40,000 graduates earned a

J.D. Thereafter, the number rose to 40,213, fluctuated above and below 40,000 for years, dropped to 37,909 in 2001–02, and grew steadily to 43,518 in 2007–08. There have been no major increases in the last fifteen years, most likely because this coincides with the last of the Generation Xers graduating college and entering professional school. This can easily change with the rise of the much larger Generation Y.

How will the economic crisis affect the career choices of Generation Y? Will the economic crisis persuade more young people to go to law school (or pursue any kind of advanced degree, for that matter)? There was a spike in enrollment from 2001 to 2005, following the last recession. Will a recession-boosted spike dovetail with the rising population of Generation Yers and result in a surge in law-school enrollment? It seems likely that the larger Generation Y will indeed increase law-school enrollment to some extent, but it is also possible that the destabilization of the legal industry may, for a while, discourage young people from pursuing legal careers.

When young people in the U.S. consider their options today, they might worry that a law degree will not return their investment. In addition to the uncertain economy and a legal industry in desperate transition, the size of their loan debt is likely to be an issue. Nearly 44,000 law students will graduate in 2009, and each graduate will be burdened by an average loan debt of $73,000, according to the American Bar

WHERE LAWYERS WORK

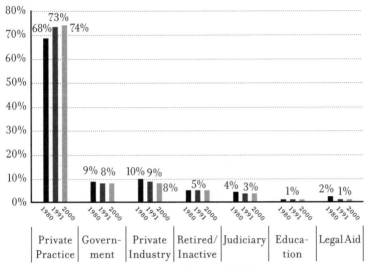

PRACTICE SETTING

Source: *The Lawyer Statistical Report,* American Bar Foundation, 1985, 1994, 2004 editions. Not pictured: "Private Association," which remained 1% for 1980, 1991 and 2000.

Association. More students are taking out loans for undergraduate education as well as graduate and professional-school educations. Aspiring lawyers have more cause than ever to worry that their dream careers might not exist five years from now. It is questionable how many of the best and the brightest young people will be willing to invest their money and time toward an uncertain future.

Part of their worry will arise from the fear that they will not recoup their investment. They might expect to earn $160,000 in a large firm, but this is increasingly unlikely. Large firms are shedding employees, laying off staff, cutting back investments, and scrambling

AGES OF LICENSED LAWYERS

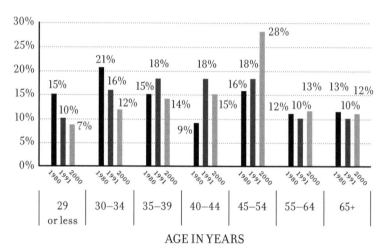

AGE IN YEARS

The graph shows the percentages of U.S. licensed lawyers of various ages. Source: *The Lawyer Statistical Report,* American Bar Foundation, 1985, 1994, 2004 editions. **Median ages: 39** in 1980, **41** in 1991, and **45** in 2000.

to revise their business plans. Even without industry turmoil, 63% of private practitioners work in small firms of two to five lawyers (see chart on page 60), earning far less than their big-firm counterparts. So those law graduates with $73,000 of debt will be far more likely to work in small firms and earn $50,000 to $75,000 a year.

And those who do manage to work in large firms will face threats to their earning capacity and their career tracks. Attrition rates even in 2006 were found to be 19% at U.S. law firms of all sizes, according to a NALP survey of the time. The survey also revealed that 80% of associates leave their firms within five years.

Causing a landslide of layoffs, the recent economic crisis has further compounded the uncertainty of law-firm careers, and lawyers today confront the daunting prospect of lifelong career opportunism. According to data from Incisive Legal Intelligence, over 13,000 lateral partners joined, left, or moved among the *American Lawyer* 200 firms between 2000 and 2005. Career opportunism has become a permanent strategy for lawyers, but tougher economic times are eliminating opportunities, as well as careers.

The demographic trends are combining with the trends in globalization, technology and business to force dynamic change in the legal industry. Over time the legal industry will come to value a person's ability to manage projects and lead people who are not under one roof. A new legal model will emerge that values people who have the ability to manage a variety of relationships, legal and otherwise, and to assemble the best talent in the best place at the best time. New legal models will emphasize the management of relationships and labor beyond the traditional partner/associate model. This is ultimately what corporate clients will value. Entrepreneurs will have to build structures to fit the new way we work, given advances in communication technology, workflow software, collaborative networks, and the global labor marketplace.

"In a down market, the reduced-hour lawyers are often the most cost effective, because they are not being paid full-time for hours not billed."

DEBORAH EPSTEIN HENRY,
Founder and President
FLEX-TIME LAWYERS LLC
PHILADELPHIA, PA

INTERVIEW..

Did you start Flex-Time Lawyers for reasons of personal experience or did you notice a shift in demographics?

It was personal to me. I was a commercial litigator in New York until 1997 when I transferred to Philadelphia. I was pregnant with my second child, and I joined a Philadelphia law firm part time. I was on partnership track, albeit a delayed track, due to my seventy-five percent schedule. Like most professional mothers, I struggled with how I could play an integral role in my kids' lives and still be successful in my career. Occasionally I had lunch with the other part-time litigators at my firm, and we talked about our challenges and what was working for us. I found these lunches to be very helpful. In 1999, I sent six emails to friends and colleagues, announcing that I was starting a group that would meet regularly and talk about work/life issues. Within days, 150 people emailed back. I was stunned. I knew I'd struck a nerve and that I was no longer alone. I've been running Flex-Time Lawyers now for ten years.

How are you taking advantage of the growing trend of flex-time lawyers as an entrepreneurial opportunity?

The different aspects of my business have grown out of each other. I started running programs in Philadelphia and New York, and I built a listserv, an online network of contacts. I would announce programs and meetings on the listserv, and the network grew. Because of the network, employers contacted me to consult and recruit. For the recruiting, they wanted me to connect them with part-time lawyers. I ran what's now called Flex-Time Lawyers for three years *pro bono* until I transitioned it into a business and no longer practiced law. Flex-Time Lawyers is a consulting firm, and I advocate work/life balance and the retention and promotion of women to law firms and law departments nationally. I don't advertise the placement part of my business, but there's not a week that goes by that an employer doesn't inquire.

What demographic trends do you see among flex-timers?

Ten years ago, my network's demographic was largely like me, a Generation X professional woman trying to be an involved mother and a successful practitioner. The demographic has grown beyond that. As an issue, work/life balance is now gender neutral and reason neutral. Both men and women are searching for work/life balance for reasons that go beyond child rearing. They have many reasons, from caring for elderly parents to pursuing music or athletics to just wanting to live a reasonable life. Both male and female Generation Y law students already know that they don't want the lifestyles of their parents. They're making work/life balance an issue in itself. The more we move work/life balance away from being a mother's issue, the more successful we will be in making change.

With the economic crisis hitting law firms and law departments, are there going to be more flex-timers who have been fired or let go?

There is a lot of concern that the first employees to be fired are those working flexible or reduced hours. However, that should not be the case. In a down market, the reduced-hour lawyers are often the most cost effective, because they are not being paid full-time for hours not billed.

One area of expertise for me is re-entry: women who have left the profession, mostly due to child rearing, for one or more years and now they're trying to get back. In the re-entry programs I participate in, I'm noticing more downsized lawyers are attending. So, the programming is being adjusted to cover lawyers who have been laid off, in addition to those re-entering the workforce or moving from full-time to flex-time. I am a consultant to the New York State Bar Association Committee on Lawyers in Transition, and we chose the name "Lawyers in Transition" to reflect the diversity of people's motivations and circumstances.

What are the advantages of flex-time lawyering?

I'm an advocate of flex-time as a win/win scenario for both the lawyers and their employers. As a consultant, I don't tell law firms that it's the right thing to do to accommodate these lawyers. In fact, I'll never use the word *accommodate*. Using flex-time is a strategy for retaining talented lawyers who would otherwise leave the firm. These are lawyers with valuable expertise, and clients today care less about the firm's employment arrangements and far more about getting better value for their legal dollar. The details of the arrangements vary from case to case, but the employment relationship has to remain financially beneficial for everyone.

What does your acronym FACTS stand for?
The adjective *part-time*, which tends be used pejoratively, is obsolete. Instead, I created the acronym FACTS, which stands for Fixed, Annualized, Core, Targeted, and Shared hours. FACTS is a means to re-jigger the law-firm billable-hour model to give work/life choices to all lawyers.

Under the FACTS methodology, all lawyers establish a yearly *target* number of hours with their supervisor and their compensation is adjusted accordingly. Once the target hours are established, the other four prongs of FACTS focus on the way work gets done. A lawyer can work a *fixed* number of hours in a predictable schedule. Or their performance can be *annualized*, meaning they might work intensely for short periods, which would be followed by time off. *Core* refers to the way lawyers might rearrange the blocks of time they work. They might work a certain core number of hours a day or week, while setting aside other time for daily or weekly commitments. And *shared* refers to job-sharing, which is more common in other industries and among legal employers other than law firms, where it is still fairly unusual. All of these alternatives require mutual flexibility and communication to make them work.

Seven

The Legal Education Trend

New ways to educate legal professionals

From online law schools to new fields of study, legal education will have to respond to the changing dynamics of the legal industry in order to prepare graduates for the new ways legal services are organized and delivered.

Legal education has to admit the changing reality of the legal workplace. It has to alter its presumptions of the practice of law as an insular profession and the business of legal services as an afterthought. The changing global workplace is altering what it means to practice law and what it means to provide legal services. The new workplace is putting pressures on legal professionals, and legal education has to find ways to inform, support and prepare people for this new world.

Legal education has to respond to all the previous trends that have been described. New information technology and collaborative software are changing the ways legal professionals work (and suggesting new ways students might learn). People will have to be more self-reliant, flexible, computer savvy, and comfortable collaborating with others using shared software applications. Graduates will have new roles beyond traditional firm partner or solo practitioner to set their sights on, like chief legal officer, legal project manager, and legal entrepreneur, all of which will require the individual to be familiar with the new models of legal providers beyond the law firm. Legal professionals may work in different relationships with their employers: as flex-timers, part-timers, and job-sharers. Or they might even work in capacities outside the typical state-licensing system (for example, as in-house corporate counsel for a global company, as CEO of an online legal-service company, or as the founder of a new type of legal-service provider, perhaps even one overseas).

Legal professionals are far more likely to work as solo practitioners or in small firms of two to five lawyers, not in mid- or large-size firms, and their success will depend on their ability to run these practices in today's world. Students need business knowledge and entrepreneurial skills sooner rather than later. It is no longer enough to equip graduates with the knowledge to pass bar exams. Graduates need business and management skills in order to thrive as practitioners. They will have to learn about contract staffing, best-shoring, and alternative providers. Even (or especially) graduates who become private practitioners in small firms can no longer afford to be ignorant about unbundling, standardization, specialization, and globalization.

Law firms of all sizes are recognizing the need for new associates to have management skills, a business background, or even entrepreneurial experience. The practice of law is becoming more technological, collaborative, sophisticated, creative, and more service-oriented. There will, therefore, be a tremendous overhaul in how firms select talent. Employers will reduce their reliance on traditional filters—like LSAT scores, law-school reputations, grades, class rankings, participation on law-review journals, and summer internships—and move toward a more complex hiring process based on a broader assessment of the graduate that gauges in many ways (such as business aptitude and project-management experience) how the individual will perform in today's environment.

Management education is key. Legal education must support students as they explore and develop legal management skills, like the expertise needed to pull together disparate resources to complete projects. Management skills are no longer important solely for managing partners. They are critical for all legal professionals. Everyone in legal services should be exposed to the big picture of how work will be managed. Education should address project management, collaboration, team work, efficiency, productivity, outsourcing, and more. To this end, it is conceivable that, in addition to expanding course instruction to cover these subjects, law schools will encourage and arrange for new internships and externships that place law students in non-traditional environments, that is, beyond law firms and into new legal providers or law-related businesses. Once employers begin to look for and value this kind of experience, students will insist on getting it.

Traditionally, lawyers worked to be rainmakers in order to pursue higher compensation. Rainmakers will be necessary roles for many lawyers to play, but wooing clients will no longer be the exclusive path to financial success. Highly skilled managers will also be highly compensated, just as they are in other sectors of the business world. They will manage people and projects effectively; they will identify the right resources at the right time; and they will provide legal services with the right cost structure. The legal professionals who excel at these skill sets will become highly desirable in the new workplace. There will be whole new tracks within law schools that educate graduates for these new roles in the business of law. These graduates will be the new leaders of tomorrow's providers and law firms.

As for today's law students, the nearly 44,000 law graduates of 2009 will have an average of $73,000 in loan debt, according to the American Bar Association. (See page 83 for a chart of law-school enrollment.) They will also emerge in the midst of a dire transition.

By February 2008, the class of 2007 was employed at a 91.9% rate, a twenty-year high (the last highest was 92% in 1988), according to a NALP report. The NALP report surveyed 186 ABA-accredited law schools, which provided information on 40,416 graduates, or 92.7% of all graduates. (They could be employed in any job, legal or non-legal; 55.5% were in private practice, while 14.1% were in business.) Sixteen percent of the employed attorneys had starting salaries of $160,000. More than twice as many (38%) had salaries of $55,000 or less. And 72% of those employed started work in firms with fifty or fewer attorneys. Median salaries for those employed in government were $50,000; in public-interest organizations, $42,000; and as judicial clerks, $48,000. (See page 122 for a salary graph.)

All that, however, was over a year ago, and a lot has happened to the economy and the legal industry since that time. Law firms have merged, gone out of business, or slashed their budgets. Associates have been laid off in droves. Partners have moved or been forced out. Legal budgets everywhere are tightening. The demand for legal services has dropped globally. Some practice areas have dried up completely. Pay rates have been frozen, and bonuses have been suspended.

Current law students have been watching the crisis unfold from within the caves of law school, but as they emerge into the light of 2009, they will be met

FROM LSAT TO J.D.

ACADEMIC YEAR	LSATS TAKEN	ABA APPLICANTS	ADMITTED APPLICANTS	ENROLLED FIRST-YEARS	J.D. OR LL.B AWARDED
2007–08	142,300	83,400	55,500	49,082	43,518
2006–07	140,000	84,000	55,500	49,100	43,920
2005–06	137,400	88,700	56,000	48,900	42,673
2004–05	145,300	95,800	56,100	48,100	40,023
2003–04	147,600	100,600	55,900	48,200	38,874
2002–03	148,000	99,500	56,800	48,900	38,605
2001–02	134,300	90,900	56,500	48,400	37,909
2000–01	109,000	77,200	51,800	45,100	38,157
1999–00	107,200	74,600	50,300	43,500	39,071
1998–99	104,200	74,400	51,300	43,200	39,455

Source: Law School Admission Council, Data Volume Summary, and ABA Law School Enrollment statistics.

with the harsh glare of an unforgiving marketplace. Most will have a traditional law-school education behind them and a new, rocky employment landscape in front of them. Their future is uncertain.

What lawyers are expected to do and how they are expected to survive have changed drastically. Legal education needs to respond quickly to prepare its graduates with more than the traditional legal education. Young people today who are thinking about law school are going to be wary of going into massive debt just for the opportunity to face such grim uncertainty. They are most likely to end up in a smaller firm making less than $55,000 a year (and working hard as a business manager to make even that). And if they work in a larger firm, they are less likely than ever to realize the traditional goal of making partner. Baby Boomers are staying put at the top positions of law firms. Associate attrition has traditionally been high due to the slow, if not stalled, tracks to partnership. In 2009, associate attrition has slowed due to the economic uncertainty. Associates are cautiously remaining with their current firms instead of risking moves to other firms. And most of all, the law firms are modifying (even abandoning) the associate/partner structure itself.

A hopeful student might be wise to take advantage of alternative means of legal education. Part-time degrees and even online part-time degrees (which are being offered by some law schools today but remain unaccredited by the ABA) might become much more attractive to future students who need to work (and offset their debt) while going to school.

The legal industry has changed and is changing. Ultimately (and very quickly), legal education must adapt in order to enable the next generation of lawyers to adapt.

"If you don't increase the numbers of minority applicants getting into law school, then all the work I'm doing with firms is going to be limited by the flow of people coming out of law school."

CHRIS JOHNSON, *Director*
GRADUATE PROGRAM IN CORPORATE LAW
AND FINANCE, THOMAS M. COOLEY LAW
SCHOOL; *Former General Counsel* OF
NORTH AMERICA FOR GENERAL MOTORS

INTERVIEW..

How has the role of general counsel changed since you started?
Globalization has brought the biggest changes. There is an overall general counsel at GM, and four other general counsel for four regions. For seven years, I was general counsel for General Motors, North America. I had responsibility for the U.S., Canada, and Mexico. When I came into the job, I had 60% of the lawyers. When I retired in November 2008, I had less than 50%. This was a result of globalization. GM was building and sending more cars into Russia, China, and India, so our legal footprint changed. The structure of the legal department followed the evolving structure of the company. Originally, the structure was regional. Cars were built in the region to sell in the region. Now we have what's known as a basket-weave structure. Engineering, manufacturing, human resources, legal, public policy, finance: they're all now working across regions to drive common processes. The effects of globalization increased the amount of work for us, but it didn't change

what we had to do in the U.S. I had less than half the lawyers, but I had 90% of the budget, because with litigation and regulation the U.S. is still a significant part of the cost structure.

How did the relationship with outside counsel evolve over the years you were at GM?

We made some changes to increase diversity and to lower cost. We were moving away from larger national firms, particularly firms in New York, and moving toward firms in Detroit and other lower-cost legal markets. We made decisions among outside counsel by using metrics like head count, budget, diversity, and the quality of legal work. In other words, I gave outside counsel certain targets to meet, and however they chose to meet them, they did what was necessary. In the patent area, rather than going to India, for example, we used retirees to work on patents, to keep costs below the rates other people were using. We took control of outside-counsel rates years ago. Firms don't raise their rates. We grant increases for good cause shown. We're also moving away from relying on the straight hourly rate. Three-quarters of our labor/employment work is based on a flat fee. That's been the case since 2003.

How did you set and track targets for diversity?

Diversity was and is one of my major focus points. We started by looking at diversity in our own legal departments and in outside law firms. We coded every lawyer by race and gender so we could track who was billing hours on our matters. We set goals for outside counsel in 2003 using this system: 20% minority and 33% women. Those were the percentages we were after for those people working for us, and for billing attributable to us. We had over 10,000 lawyers working for GM as outside counsel, and we just couldn't monitor that many lawyers. So we used a billing system to

MINORITY LAW-SCHOOL EXPERIENCE, 2007

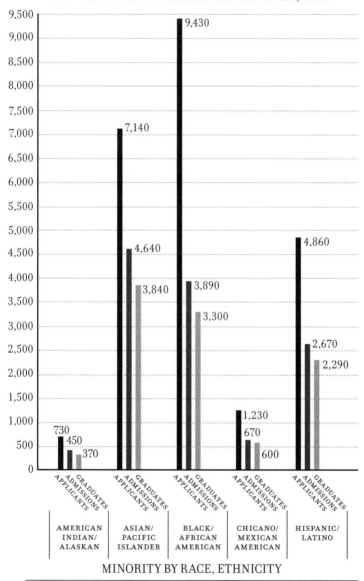

MINORITY BY RACE, ETHNICITY

Source: Law School Admission Council, Data Volume Summary, figures rounded. According to the ABA, the percentage of law-school
graduates who are minorities has more than doubled from 10% during
the late 1980s to 23% today.

track it by code and produce reports to show how we
and the firms were doing. So when Lawyer X filled
out time sheets, the report would code X as a partner,
associate, woman, African American, etc. It was done
automatically. No one had to fill out a separate report.

What did the first reports show?

The first reports in 2003 were lower than we expected. In
the next three years, we went from 10% to 15% minority
percentages, and women grew from 20% to 26%. We
didn't get to the absolute numbers we were looking for,
but we made significant improvements.

Was there a particular obstacle to increasing the percentages?

Firms had complained about the low retention rates of
minority and women associates. So in 2007 we did
something unique. Because of high turnover among
associates, we were concerned that we were just paying
to train associates and then watching them leave. In
response, we designed a mentor program. We identified
three to five up-and-coming associates and got them
more involved in the GM account at the firm. We tried
to align associates more closely with us by mentoring
them to become leaders on the GM account. Firms really
embraced this concept for the same reason we did. We
were encouraging these men and women to become
leaders of the future. This would increase the diversity of
the firm and of our outside counsel at the same time. The
program just started in North America, and it's had very
good reception. We're trying it with six of our biggest
firms.

Have you explored ways to increase minority applications to law schools?

If you don't increase the numbers of minority applicants
getting into law school, then all the work I'm doing with

MINORITIES IN LAW FIRMS, 2007

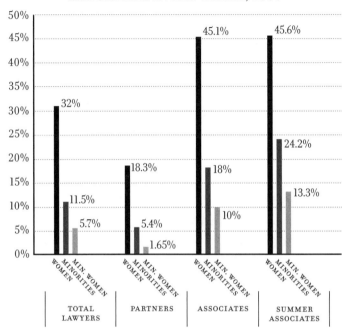

The graph shows the percentages of women, minorities, and minority women in private U.S. law firms. Source: *2007–08 NALP Directory of Legal Employers.* In a 2007 VAULT survey of 193 law firms, nearly 10% did not consider conducting an internal diversity assessment to be a priority.

firms is going to be limited by the flow of people coming out of law school. So we've started at the high-school level. We have pipeline initiatives, in particular the Street Law Program, which educates inner-city students about legal careers and encourages them to be lawyers. We've been doing this since 2004. We're working with the Detroit and Pontiac school systems. These are intensive. We go into classrooms and stage day-long mock trials. We have internships over the summer. A number of kids who have gone through the program are now in college, and whether or not they become lawyers, these are kids who have gone to college who otherwise wouldn't have.

The 7 Trends, in Dynamic Relation

The trends are interdependent. It is often difficult to tease them apart. The deeper you investigate them, the more they seem to be part of a whole. Actions cause reactions, and trends build upon each other. The pressure on the legal industry to become more businesslike is a common theme among all these trends: globalization, efficiency, information, people. The movement toward law as a business will emphasize the importance of entrepreneurial thinking. Those who resist creative thinking and insist on business as usual risk being left behind in the limbo of yesterday. Those who face the facts, consider the trends, and embrace entrepreneurship will be ready for the work of tomorrow.

Everything Builds in One Direction

Most people agree that industries tend to go in cycles. My observation over the past decade is that economic cycles (and market-opportunity time frames) are shortening. As an entrepreneur, I respond constantly to what is next while I make sure I am not getting too far ahead of myself. If I do the same thing mindlessly for the next five years without innovation and without tweaking the business model, I may be profitable, but I am dying, even if the financial numbers do not show it yet. Soon enough, they will, and then it will be too late. Take the automotive industry. You could argue that they ignored the external market changes in favor of enjoying their internal business success. While a lot was happening in the global business world and even right in their own backyard, they were satisfied with their success. And today they are paying the price.

I read the business magazines, the journals, the newspapers. I pay close attention to what the trends look like in the legal industry. I read from other services tracking this industry. And I am always asking, "What does it mean for me?" You can learn a lot from history, but you also have to look at today's demographics and social trends. These trends will affect how business will be done in the future. What are today's numbers telling us about tomorrow?

Without doubt, today's numbers are telling us that change is coming rapidly to the legal industry. It is inevitable. It has happened in other industries, it is accelerating in the legal industry, and it is going to happen faster than those within the legal industry assume it will. Why? Because the legal industry is one of the last industries undergoing the change. It has happened to other professional services like accounting and finance, and the pressure is coming from business clients, through general counsel who hire law firms and from the corporations who are already doing business globally and, of course, already under pressure to deliver goods and services better, faster and cheaper. The wheels are greased, in other words. And this means that those in the legal industry need to innovate. Law firms need to modify their business model. And part of what they need to modify is their very mindset.

Business always changes. It reacts to technology and to consumer demand. It leverages information. It takes advantage of opportunities to compete. But law firms have been historically very different. They are based on a professional model. And most firms loathe change. As the legal industry feels the pressure of the market, law firms will realize that their privileges have suddenly become bad habits. Some will get caught flat-footed, because they did not see change coming so fast. Others will see that change is coming, but they will not know what to do about it.

Overall, everything builds in one direction. And the big picture is this:

The pressure to provide services better, faster and cheaper is forcing the legal industry to behave more like a business in an ever-changing economy. Law firms will have to sacrifice the premium pricing of the billable hour in order to improve efficiency and productivity. Law firms will have to become more flexible in their pricing models and strategies. They will have to listen much more closely to their clients and customers. They will have to offer a variety of pricing options, including billable hours, fixed fees, performance-based fees, task-based fees, and other alternatives that take advantage of temporary staffing, standardization, unbundling, outsourcing, and more.

Rising Associate Salaries

Starting salaries for first-year associates, which were steady between 2000 and 2005, soared in 2006 and 2007. High starting salaries lure top candidates, so the theory goes, and having the top candidates means having the best lawyers, which justifies the highest hourly rates.

How high can they go? To $160,000 a year, so far.

This new record started at top New York firms in 2007. Other firms, like Orrick Herrington & Sutcliffe, followed New York's lead. And then Texas (Vinson & Elkins in Houston) and Washington firms followed suit. Even firms with fewer than 400 lawyers matched the $160,000 starting salary, including Crowell & Moring (Washington), Townsend and Townsend and Crew (San Francisco), and Munger Tolles & Olson (Los Angeles). Others include the 576-attorney firm of Perkins Coie (Seattle) and the 477-attorney firm Mintz Levin Cohn Ferris Glosky and Popeo (Boston).

The "war for talent," as the practice is often called, is mainly fought among the largest firms, those whose business model depends on hiring those who graduate at the tops of their classes with the most honors. (About 40,000 students graduate from law school in the U.S. every year.) The salaries are not rising nearly as fast for associates in medium to small firms. A 2007 *Of Counsel* article noted the widening gap in first-year pay between *American Lawyer* 100 firms and mid-size firms and went on to suggest that mid-size firms do more to recruit third- and fourth-year associates who have become disillusioned with large firms. (Today, laid-off lawyers present another attractive, and significant, talent pool.)

How many associates are there? Major firms employ one associate for every partner, while lawyers in medium and smaller firms rely on fewer associates. The overall ratio of lawyers to partners is 2.19 (one associate for every two lawyers), according to a recent analysis of the *2006–07 NALP Directory of Legal Employers,* which represents over 132,413 lawyers in more than 1,500 law offices nationwide, primarily in firms of more than 100 lawyers.

The trend of skyrocketing salaries upsets those in the business world, especially general counsel who are trying to contain costs.

"Historically, law-firm profitability is largely based on annual fee increases rather than law firms improving their 'quality and value proposition' through internal efforts at standardization, coordination, and effective use of technology," said Jonathan Oviatt, general counsel for Mayo Clinic, quoted in an article in *The National Law Journal* on August 13, 2007. "I expect in-house counsel will increasingly object to annual fee increases proposed by outside counsel, especially if we do not see outside counsel focusing on efficiency in a manner comparable to what we live with on a daily basis."

The trend is unsustainable. Firms are pressuring associates by increasing billable-hour requirements, as well as other methods. Firms are less able to cut costs in response to client demand. Firms are also in a quandary when it comes to training and retaining associates. According to NALP statistics, nearly 80% of associates leave their firms by the fifth year. Firms invest heavily in training associates only to see them leave, despite the higher salaries. Clients complain about the turnover rate, because they are essentially paying to retrain new associates. In 2009, major U.S.-based law firms are holding the line on first-year starting salaries, are reducing associate bonus payouts, and have begun looking at performance-based compensation models. A struggling economy and less work were cited as the main factors in keeping salaries in check.

DISTRIBUTION OF FULL-TIME SALARIES OF THE CLASS OF 2006 LAW GRADUATES

% OF SALARIES

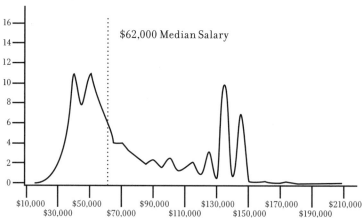

ANNUAL SALARY

Source: NALP The Association for Legal Career Professionals

SALARIES FOR FIRST-YEAR LAW-FIRM ASSOCIATES

	2006	2007

FIRMS OF ALL SIZES

MEDIAN FIRST-YEAR ASSOCIATE SALARY:	$105,000	$113,000

FIRMS WITH 25 OR FEWER LAWYERS

MEDIAN FIRST-YEAR ASSOCIATE SALARY:	$67,000	$68,000

FIRMS WITH 501+ LAWYERS

MEDIAN FIRST-YEAR ASSOCIATE SALARY:	$135,000	$145,000

FOR COMPARISON

AVERAGE SALARY, STAFF ATTORNEY	$98,000
AVERAGE SALARY, LAW CLERK	$24,000—$50,000
AVERAGE SALARY, PROSECUTOR	$46,000

MEDIAN FIRST-YEAR ASSOCIATE SALARIES OVER TIME[*]

FIRM SIZE # ATTYS	1999	2001	2003[†]	2005
2-25	$51,000	$60,000	$59,000	$67,500
26-50	$57,500	$70,500	$71,000	$80,000
51-100	$67,000	$75,900	$80,000	$83,000
101-250	$70,000	$90,000	$85,000	$86,000
251+	$85,000	$110,200	$107,000	$110,000
251+ (NY)	$96,000	$125,000	$125,000	$125,000
251+ (L.A.)	$92,000	$125,000	$125,000	$125,000

Source: *NALP Associate Salary Survey 2007.* Numbers are based on 679 offices providing salary information as of April 1, 2007. One quarter of respondents were from firms of 50 or fewer lawyers while 32% of firms had more than 500 lawyers. *Long-term salary statistics from *NALP Associate Salary Surveys.* †Median salaries declined in this year due to a different pool of respondents. Salaries at any one firm did not decline.

The economic crisis and global recession of 2009 are putting a dramatic halt to associate starting salaries. In the near term, *NLJ* 250 law firms will reduce first-year associate salaries, according to how these firms reposition themselves in the newly developing legal marketplace.

The war for talent is a remnant of the traditional price structure, sustainable only with the premium pricing of the billable hour. The top firms can still afford to do this in a profession where price is a proxy for quality, but other firms will need to resort to more flexible compensation structures to achieve the efficiency demanded by their clients.

Time is Running Out on Time-Based Billing

Alternative pricing has been around for two decades, mostly as fixed fees insisted upon by corporate and institutional clients. The legal industry has been isolated from the kind of serious pressure to cut costs that has affected manufacturing, the service industry, and even professions like accounting, finance, and, to some extent, health care. While those industries have scrambled to cut costs and improve efficiency without sacrificing quality, law firms have been able to pick and choose alternative strategies at their leisure. They have done so by relying on their pricing hallmark, the billable hour.

The billable hour is attractive. It is familiar. It is safe. And it is easy. Firms are risk-averse entities and prefer to avoid experimentation. Why fix the billable hour if it works so well for them as is? They do not have to quantify the value of their services up front, the way other businesses and professions have to do. They can simply charge for more hours at premium rates.

Law firms have relied on the exact same business model, based on the billable hour, for about fifty years. "The 1960s marked the coming of age of the billable hour," reported an ABA Commission in 2002. The model was created to address antitrust concerns, assist lawyers with managing productivity, and alleviate client confusion about how fees were determined. But the billable hour, the Commission wrote, "is fundamentally about quantity over quality, repetition over creativity. With no gauge for intangibles such as productivity, creativity, knowledge or technological advancements, the billable-hours model is a counterintuitive measure of value. Alternatives that encourage efficiency and improve processes not only increase profits and provide early resolution of legal matters, but are less likely to garner ethical concerns."

Every lawyer by now has heard the complaints about the billable hour, maybe even been the one complaining. But the short and interesting history of the billable hour can be told this way. As far back as the early 1900s, a lawyer charged a reasonable fee according to a variety of factors, including time, labor, skill, custom, experience, speed of performance, and reputation. But the profession was opaque, sometimes deliberately so, and clients were often confused by the law as much as by how fees were determined. So they paid gratefully and mostly without complaint. Then, informally, lawyers tracked their hours. By the 1950s, most firms realized they could make more money billing by the hour. By the 1960s, the transition was total and routine. Firms have enjoyed the billable hour virtually unchallenged until, more or less, today.

Compared to companies in other industries, law firms have a disproportionate percentage of highly compensated employees. Over the past decade, large law firms have generated tremendous profits. Law-firm partners have been highly compensated. Annual income can reach seven figures. This profitability is mainly due to the premium pricing of the billable hour, in which all services are valued at the same rate. Clients today know more about the business of law. They are less confused, because the law is less opaque. Clients, especially large, corporate clients, are skeptical of the billable hour because it is virtually extinct in the business world. They understand that technology—especially time-tracking and document-management software programs—combined with other trends have rendered the pricing of legal services susceptible to improvement. Certain tasks can be isolated and quantified. Those original factors used in the 1900s are coming back into play, but this time in a very different world, one of incredible technology, legal transparency, and global business practices. Time can now be one factor among many.

The stage has been set for alternative pricing, and more firms than ever are choosing to test the waters. For years, firms have been experimenting with contingency fees, flat fees, result-based premiums, retainers, and even stock in exchange for services. But the ABA has noted that the experiments with alternative fees, which have included bill auditing, task-based billing, Total Quality Management, and others, have yet to unseat the billable hour as the standard practice for most billing. The reason is simple. Law firms have not experienced enough external market pressure to change. Due to the financial and economic crisis of 2008–09, a serious and intense pressure is now being felt.

While many firms and clients have experimented with alternative pricing, the reality is that the billable hour is, for the time being, still king. Altman Weil's 2008 survey of 115 general counsel found that 83% still paid their outside counsel by hourly billing almost exclusively. In a 2006 survey, 55 out of 138 corporate counsel said they did not use any alternative-fee arrangements. They paid legal fees solely by the hour. Forty-eight corporate counsel said from 1–20% of fee arrangements were alternative, and about 14 corporate counsel said 21–40% were alternative. In a 2005 law-firm management survey, all 63 respondents said they had used alternative pricing and that it was somewhat to very successful. What mainly constituted "alternative," however, was the contingency fee and the fixed rate. At one point, Cisco set aside 70% (about $125 million) of their annual legal budget to fixed rates for litigation and corporate and securities work.

The times are changing. Corporate clients, who are under so much pressure to compete, are thinking about ways to cut the costs of legal services. The largest corporations, those with $5 billion in annual revenue, are spending $877,000 per lawyer on legal services in a year, according to a 2006 survey of 138 companies, 33 of which were in the largest category. Overall, the legal costs of corporations rose 8% in one year, from 2004 to 2005.

To reduce costs, companies are doing two notable things: increasing in-house counsel and decreasing outside counsel. According to a 2007 survey, the number of in-house counsel rose significantly in each of the past three years, from 2.93 lawyers per billion dollars of annual corporate revenue in 2004, to 3.49 lawyers in 2005, to 3.52 lawyers in 2006. At the same time, general counsel are feeling the pressure to reduce costs. In a 2005 *Inside Counsel* survey, general counsel agreed that reducing costs was the most important thing law firms could do. And the most recent surveys in 2009 suggest that over 75% of general counsel will be asked to make immediate budget cuts. General counsel are reducing costs by a variety of means, including reducing the number of outside counsel by as much as 80%.

This process is in its infancy. Major corporations still use, on average, over 120 firms. The smallest corporations use less than ten. According to Altman Weil's "Legal Profession Trends and Outlook," a 2007 report based on interviews with two dozen leaders of the legal profession, lawyers have begun to complain about the convergence process, claiming that increased pricing pressures are driving them out of participating in competitive bidding, that customers expect greater value for their dollar, and that companies are now asking firms to "articulate and quantify" the benefits of their services. The convergence process shocks lawyers who are used to simply increasing rates to improve profitability. Now clients are demanding that they increase productivity and efficiency.

The recent economic crisis is accelerating the demand for change.

Taking Billing to Task: Introduction to Unbundling

The billable hour can be applied to any service a lawyer provides. A lawyer can charge similar rates for very disparate tasks. A high-priced lawyer charges a high hourly rate whether talking with a client, filing a motion, or delegating research to an associate. In fact, a lawyer rarely works alone. A lawyer relies on staff, from law clerks to paralegals; on firm libraries and research assistants; on colleagues; and on associates who might research briefs and memos, organize meetings, and prepare documents according to existing templates. The client will see a bill itemizing many of these mechanical tasks and the times it took to complete them, which is multiplied by the lawyer's hourly rate to generate the fee.

Today, many of these tasks are being taken out from under the protective cover of the hourly rate and submitted to pricing that more accurately reflects the value of the task to the client-customer. Once a task can be identified and delegated, it can be priced more accurately (here, the lawyer cringes because "more accurately" inevitably means "more cheaply," while the businessperson cheers because "more accurately"

> **"Running a business based on what is convenient for the provider is a luxury that only monopolies have. It is a foreign concept for most of your clients, who are focused on customers and the market."**
>
> —Mark Usellis, "Resisting the Urge to Merge,"
> *Legal Management*, November/December 2006

Attractions of the Billable Hour

Simplifies billing

Easy to understand

Applicable to all kinds of services

Increases lawyer profitability quickly

Minimizes transaction costs involved when otherwise making judgments about the value of a service

Increases clarity and precision in tracking work when only one variable (time) involved

The hard numbers of hours worked resists client criticism

An easy proxy index by which to rate attorney quality

Disadvantages of the Billable Hour

Incapable of distinguishing value and quality of service

Tied to reputation and experience of attorney rather than value to client of the service

Increases associate attrition

Discourages *pro bono* work

Unpredictable cost for client

Unreflective of value of service

A proxy measure of the value of a task

Penalizes efficient lawyer

Discourages client/attorney communication

Encourages skipping steps

Discourages use of technology

Encourages time-sheet padding

Encourages competition on hourly rates

means the market is at work). In some cases, the task can be standardized, that is, rendered standard throughout the industry, consisting of the same basic elements no matter what firm or lawyer fulfills the task. This process is often referred to as unbundling.

A task can be delegated to staff within the firm. It can also be delegated to someone outside the firm. The general term for this is *outsourcing*. Certain tasks can be outsourced to providers outside the firm or company but in the same country. This distinction is important because when tasks are outsourced outside the country, it is called "offshore outsourcing." Businesses have been outsourcing tasks offshore for years now. The reasons for outsourcing are often cost savings, expertise, and speed. Offshoring, by contrast, occurs when a business relocates not discrete tasks but entire activities out of the country. The motivations for offshoring are similar: to improve efficiency, lower labor costs, and reach new customers.

Law firms have also been outsourcing for years, but they have been outsourcing non-law-related tasks, generally in the realm of administration, finance, and information technology. Firms have outsourced their libraries, support services like data processing and copying, as well as back-office support services, including offshore outsourcing of financial and accounting services, presentation-preparation services, and litigation-support services. Because

The Billable Hour: Requirements, Actuals & Totals

HOURS ARE GIVEN PER LAWYER PER YEAR	2005	2006
FIRMS OF ALL SIZES		
REQUIRED BILLABLE HOURS (1,085 FIRMS):	1,886	1,887
ACTUAL BILLABLE HOURS (791 FIRMS):	1,848	1,842
TOTAL HOURS WORKED (690, 701 FIRMS):	2,065	2,065
FIRMS WITH 50 OR FEWER LAWYERS		
REQUIRED BILLABLE HOURS (99, 104 FIRMS):	1,949	1,819
ACTUAL BILLABLE HOURS (106 FIRMS):	1,823	1,800
TOTAL HOURS WORKED (99 FIRMS):	1,949	1,940
FIRMS WITH 51–100 LAWYERS		
REQUIRED BILLABLE HOURS (132, 123 FIRMS):	1,849	1,851
ACTUAL BILLABLE HOURS (100 FIRMS):	1,839	1,842
TOTAL HOURS WORKED (85 FIRMS):	2,008	2,007
FIRMS WITH 101–250 LAWYERS		
REQUIRED BILLABLE HOURS (246, 241 FIRMS):	1,864	1,871
ACTUAL BILLABLE HOURS (197 FIRMS):	1,840	1,836
TOTAL HOURS WORKED (167 FIRMS):	2,042	2,037
FIRMS WITH 251–500 LAWYERS		
REQUIRED BILLABLE HOURS (329, 310 FIRMS):	1,901	1,903
ACTUAL BILLABLE HOURS (217 FIRMS):	1,869	1,862
TOTAL HOURS WORKED (187 FIRMS):	2,100	2,097
FIRMS WITH 501–700 LAWYERS		
REQUIRED BILLABLE HOURS (78, 114 FIRMS):	1,890	1,889
ACTUAL BILLABLE HOURS (65 FIRMS):	1,807	1,798
TOTAL HOURS WORKED (60 FIRMS):	2,143	2,140
FIRMS WITH 701+ LAWYERS		
REQUIRED BILLABLE HOURS (200, 193 FIRMS):	1,944	1,940
ACTUAL BILLABLE HOURS (106 FIRMS):	1,873	1,880
TOTAL HOURS WORKED (103 FIRMS):	2,147	2,174

Source: 2006–07 and 2007–08 editions of the *NALP Directory of Legal Employers.* Numbers of firms providing statistics for each measurable are indicated, for example, as "90 firms."

these tasks can be unbundled, and entire activities separated from the firm, they can be outsourced to third-party service providers located either in the country or overseas. The legal industry is no stranger to the unbundling of tasks, to outsourcing, or even to offshore outsourcing, but it is having a harder time befriending the unbundling, outsourcing, and offshore outsourcing of *law*-related tasks.

In the next three years, we will see corporations focus on shrinking their legal budgets by unbundling tasks to be performed at lower hourly rates. Then they will focus on making their legal expenditures more predictable by moving these unbundled tasks from hourly rates to fixed fees.

From Unbundling to Outsourcing

Today *outsourcing* functions as a kind of code word. It can stand as shorthand for a variety of concepts, from the rise of software call centers to the loss of jobs to overseas workers. At bottom, though, it is just another way of expressing a very familiar concept: the division of labor.

Within a law firm, many people perform different tasks related to the overall mission of providing legal services to clients. But why? Why can't one person do it all? Take the solo practitioner responsible for every aspect of the practice, from answering phones and paying utility bills to filing motions and arguing cases in court. Now explode that solo practice into a diagram of its component parts. Imagine something like a one-room multi-function office exploded into a multi-room law firm, each office now housing one of those functions. The solo lawyer is a jack of all trades, but the law firm divides up the trades and assigns them to individual jacks, including managing partners, senior partners, junior partners, associates, clerks, paralegals, legal assistants, accountants, human resources, and more. This is old news, of course, but as a mental exercise, it is useful to revisit what is so familiar. We divide up work into jobs, and jobs into tasks, and we consider it so natural we do not even notice it anymore.

This division is what makes unbundling, contract staffing, and outsourcing possible. The many tasks of the solo practitioner have been unbundled and assigned to other workers, like paralegals, law clerks, and legal assistants. The law firm's internal non-legal tasks can be outsourced to workers outside the firm, as has been the case with payroll services, accounting, administration, and information technology. For legal matters, the law firm can hire local temporary staff and contract attorneys, some to work within the firm, others to work outside it.

Explode the outsourcing law firm again, this time beyond national borders, and you see how the movement to offshore outsourcing is simply another step in a progression that began with nothing more dramatic than a solo practitioner hiring a law clerk—and now that solo practitioner can hire a law clerk in India or Israel. The more things change, the more they stay the same—albeit in different time zones.

The motivations for the division of labor, the unbundling of tasks, the use of contract staffing, and outsourcing are business motivations. They are more efficient. They are more productive. Workers can hone their skills and become experts in their tasks. And larger organizations, like law firms and corporations, can pay their employees proportionally, according to market rates for their labor.

Legal Outsourcing

General Electric was one of the first companies to send law-related work to India. "There are lots of opportunities to use foreign lawyers in place of outside counsel or other lawyers at a lower cost structure," said Suzanne Hawkins, senior counsel at GE, commenting in 2004. GE created an in-house legal department, staffing it with Indian lawyers and paralegals, in India in 2001, and its plastics division reportedly saved half a million dollars. By 2002, the savings had increased by an estimated 40%.

Microsoft outsourced limited patent-research work in 2004 to India. DuPont uses Indian lawyers to draft patent applications. A host of law firms were

LAW-RELATED TASKS TO BE OUTSOURCED

Law-related tasks that are most easily unbundled and outsourced often include the kind of work done usually by paralegals, law clerks, and associates.

CODING OF LEGAL DOCUMENTS FOR ELECTRONIC STORAGE: INDEX, ANNOTATE, AND TRANSFER INTO ELECTRONIC DATABASE.

DOCUMENT REVIEW, PROOFREADING

REVIEW OF CONFIDENTIALITY AGREEMENTS, PROCUREMENT CONTRACTS, BASIC VENDOR AGREEMENTS.

DRAFTING OF LEGAL DOCUMENTS

DRAFTING OF CONTRACTS, AGREEMENTS AND BRIEFS

DOCUMENT MANAGEMENT

LITIGATION SUPPORT, INCLUDING DISCOVERY RESEARCH, BRIEF RESEARCH, AND WRITING

MORTGAGE PROCESSING

STANDARD LICENSING AGREEMENTS

DRAFTING WILLS

DRAFTING IMMIGRATION-LAW FORMS

PREPARING SUMMARIES OF CASE HISTORIES

LEGAL RESEARCH

PATENT RESEARCH

PATENT APPLICATION DRAFTING

CORPORATE TRANSACTIONAL SERVICES

LEGAL CODING

LEGAL TRANSCRIPTION

early adopters of outsourcing law-related work to India, namely: Milbank Tweed Hadley & McCloy; Baker & McKenzie; Allen & Overy; and the patent firm Finnegan Henderson. Medium and smaller firms are outsourcing as well. The Washington, D.C., law firm Venable uses Indian companies to draft patent applications (a licensed U.S. lawyer or registered patent agent is not needed to write the patent application, although only registered agents can deal with the U.S. Patent and Trademark Office;

patent research and drafting might cost $10,000 in the U.S. but half that in India). "All our clients are medium and small law firms," says Gururaj Potnis of Manthan Services, an Indian company that performs outsourcing work for clients in the U.S. and UK. In 2004, even the publishing corporation West opened offices in India, where Indian lawyers prepare synopses of American court rulings.

In legal services, outsourcing is currently in what some commentators have called a "mass-piloting" stage. Firms are giving it a try and watching to see what happens. In 2005, there were approximately twenty offshore legal-service companies. If firms wanted to try offshore outsourcing then, they had limited choices, and many firms went through intermediary companies to vet those third-party providers. Two years later, in the spring of 2007, there were sixty legal-service companies ready to perform legal outsourcing work. Today, there are over one hundred providers.

Outsourcing remains a nascent industry. So it is tough to know exactly how many Indian lawyers perform outsourcing work for American firms. One report claims 1,800 Indians work in this sector today, and by 2010, there will be 24,000. Another report says the current number is less than 12,000, and by 2015, there will be 79,000. Other estimates range even more, as do estimates about the revenues at stake.

An often-quoted 2005 study by Forrester Research predicted the value of legal outsourcing work to India to rise from $80 million in 2005 to $4 billion by 2015. Just for some quick perspective, there were 185,000 U.S. legal-service providers in 2004; the number of employees, over 1.2 million. And the revenue for U.S. legal services, according to the U.S. Census, was $221 billion in 2005, having grown steadily and substantially from $154 billion in 1999.

General counsel are more likely than their law-firm counterparts to try offshore outsourcing. For one thing, the people down the hall in other departments of the corporation are outsourcing. Why shouldn't they try it? Other corporate departments have increased efficiency though outsourcing, capturing savings in labor costs while maintaining quality. In the corporate world, outsourcing is a proven strategy. Also, general counsel already outsource work to third parties, including law firms, in this country. They know the game plan. They may need different strategies to supervise the work of offshore outsourcers, but they know what is required of them.

"What is exciting for general counsel is that they can now act like the rest of the corporation and think about executing business processes on a global basis," said Raymond Bayley, CEO of Novus Law, which outsources work to lawyers in India, as quoted in a February 2007 article in *Inside Counsel*.

As for the ethics of outsourcing, as Yogi Berra said, it is déjà vu all over again. State and local bar associations have begun issuing ethics opinions on whether outsourcing is legal and what guidelines should be followed when outsourcing law-related work. Back in 1988, however, the issue was not outsourcing; it was contract staffing.

Temporary staffing is used in the legal industry for the same reasons it is used in any industry. Temporary workers replace employees who go on vacation, take maternity leave, or depart the company permanently. A temporary worker is a stopgap until the employee returns or the company finds a new replacement employee (which may sometimes turn out to be the temporary worker). Contract staffing in the legal industry grew over time to be utilized as a matter of course. Firms could control costs by staffing only as needed for large or urgent matters. Contract lawyers could take on unbundled tasks or perform highly specialized tasks. Smaller firms could take on larger matters—and compete with larger firms—by using contract staffing for a short term of labor-intensive work or by working with a contract attorney with a certain skill set or narrow expertise. Individual attorneys, for personal reasons or lifestyle preferences, elected to work on a contractual basis for the benefits of flexibility and control.

In 1988, the ABA issued an opinion allowing for and addressing the ethics of contract lawyers. In 2000, the ABA confirmed that, with certain restrictions, markups or surcharges were also ethical—that is, charging the client the attorney's hourly rate when the contract lawyer performed the work more cheaply. Today, many law firms and legal providers employ contract attorneys and temporary legal staff routinely. In 2008, a *National Law Journal* survey found that 240 of the *NLJ* 250 law firms employed 5,803 part-time attorneys and 3,870 temporary attorneys.

After contract staffing, the hot issue became outsourcing. Here is a short excerpt from a 2005 article in *Small Firm Business:*

> Ten or fifteen years ago when domestic companies started popping up to provide contract attorneys, legal academics and state bar officials screamed that the service was per se unethical. But all the shouting fell by the wayside when no one made an issue of the practice. Daly [Mary Daly, legal ethics expert and dean of St. John's University School of Law in New York] thinks there's a good chance that offshoring legal work will also fade as an issue of contention.

During the time the ABA remained silent on outsourcing, three local bar associations (Los Angeles, San Diego, and New York) issued guidelines advising lawyers on how to outsource law-related work, in particular about what fees to charge and when and if they had to inform clients, according to a 2007 article in *The National Law Journal.*

In 2008, the ABA finally expressed support for legal outsourcing. Ethics Opinion 08-451 allows for sending some legal work overseas, as long as U.S. attorneys preserve client confidences and the attorney-client privilege. The advisory insists that lawyers properly vet overseas workers to make sure they are trained and competent. Billing should also be reasonable. The ABA acknowledged that outsourcing can reduce legal costs and enable smaller firms to handle larger matters.

I started a contract-lawyer staffing company in 1993. The ABA's 1988 ethics opinion on contract lawyers set the course for me. Since 1988, it has taken twenty years to really see full-scale implementation of the contract-lawyer model. With outsourcing, the cycle will be accelerated. It might take only five to seven years.

Firms wary of outsourcing tend to be concerned about security, confidentiality, and the protection of client information. These concerns have been raised in other industry sectors, like accounting and finance, and they have been addressed. This means once these concerns are met in the legal industry, there will be no excuses. The race will be on.

Globalization and LPO

The word *globalization* is used to describe all sorts of phenomena, from the political to the economic, from deregulation to free-trade agreements, from the manufacture of Chinese toys to the transport of South American coffee beans.

When it refers to trade, globalization is not new at all. Trade is as old as human civilization, when tribes first exchanged furs and beads, grains and tools. Trade among nations is as old as the nations themselves. So it is strange that journalists today so often act as if China and India were discovered in the 1980s. For hundreds of years, until the late nineteenth century, China and India were the world's two largest economies. Not Britain. Not the United States. Who dominated global trade? China and India did.

It was, however, in the 1980s that the modern concept of globalization was created. Western business interests wanted to expand globally. The U.S. government helped them do it. The new policy priorities were deregulation, privatization, and free trade, and they soon became the key words for the missions of the World Bank, the International Monetary Fund, and the World Trade Organization. Markets were opened. Capital moved all over the world.

For those who remember, this historic moment should bring back memories of U.S. President Ronald Reagan and British Prime Minister Margaret Thatcher, the "Washington Consensus," and the collapse of the Soviet Union. It was a moment as convulsive and painful for many countries' economies as it was celebratory for Western economies. Russia's economy succumbed to corruption and chaos, while the economies of Mexico, Argentina, and Thailand plummeted. For its part, China remained protectionist and highly regulated (and to an extent remains so today), while India, in a bout of nationalist spirit after independence from English colonialism in 1947, threw up protectionist barriers and successfully grew its economy in the 1980s until a crisis in 1991 forced it to open its borders to international trade. And the U.S., it should be noted, is no stranger to protectionist policies, such as its subsidies for agribusiness.

The global expansion of trade has never been and is not today a simple story. Book after book has been written on the fits and starts of the past several decades of modern globalization, on its highs and lows, its winners and losers. I touch very lightly on all this to emphasize that globalization is far more than just a code word for outsourcing. Anyone in legal services today has a lot more to consider than just figuring out a way to save a few dollars by outsourcing document review to a lawyer in India. What is far more important to understand is that the future of legal services is global, complex, and uncertain. Entrepreneurs in this industry have to be prepared to completely revise their business models, to pick and choose their strategies very carefully, and to adapt to changing conditions at home and on the other side of the world.

Financial Services

Today, we cannot help but look back at the history of financial services through the looking glass of the global financial crisis of 2008–09. As of this writing, the economic situation remains unstable. The future is uncertain. But it is still worth looking at the globalization of financial services, because the industry provides a glimpse into the possible future of legal services. Legal services will experience many of the same growing pains that financial services has endured, and perhaps, by way of lessons learned, legal entrepreneurs may avoid the worst of those pains.

The financial-services industry was there at the beginning of modern globalization. Industry leaders in finance, telecommunications, and transportation lobbied the U.S. government to pursue policies supporting globalization. Today, twenty-five years later, financial markets are interconnected and interdependent (and accessible via the internet), and multinational corporations have offices across the globe. As for outsourcing, the industries of banking, finance and insurance make up about 40% of the outsourcing market, far and away the dominant sector. The technology industry makes up 15%, telecom 17%, and manufacturing 12%.

The question for companies in these industries is not whether or not to outsource, but how to do it well. Outsourcing is a given, one tool among many for keeping a company competitive. Over half of all financial institutions employ a mix of outsourcing and offshoring strategies. They may outsource some activities within the same country, outsource other activities outside the country, establish offshore facilities of the company, and even then outsource some tasks of that offshore site to yet another third-party vendor in a third country. The overall business strategy becomes crucial, and managing all the relations between offshore operations and outsourcers will make or break the company.

Offshore sites (also called "captive operations") of financial companies have been shown to achieve savings of up to 50%, as opposed to 38% achieved using third-party outsourcers. This difference may be due to better and more consistent management. Because of management turnover and lax culture, some facilities suffer from offshoring fatigue and slip in performance, failing to sustain their savings. To keep their operations viable, financial institutions have to manage their outsourcing relationships closely. They have to make sure their third-party outsourcers are complying with security and privacy regulations. For their offshore facilities, they have to create and maintain a strong corporate culture to combat the effects of staff turnover and offshore fatigue. A strong corporate culture should foster communication and reward employee performance. And companies have to resist complacency. They cannot sit back and hope to reap cost savings indefinitely. They have to balance their efforts to cut costs with long-term investment in the growth and continued innovation of the company.

The past decades of globalization in financial services and IT have created hot-spot cities in India, eastern Europe, and Russia. Most offshoring and outsourcing efforts have taken place in cities like Hyderabad, Bangalore, Delhi, Mumbai, Budapest, Prague, and Moscow. Third-party vendors have sprung up, and global companies like IBM, GE, Microsoft, American Express, Hewlett-Packard and others have built offshore facilities, corporate parks, and to an extent invested in infrastructure.

Young people have flocked to these cities, and populations have increased. But as these hot spots have grown, they have encountered new problems. Fidelity Investments, Nokia, and Microsoft have built facilities in Gurgaon, a suburb of New Delhi, spurring commercial and retail development, but the suburb now suffers traffic congestion, power outages, and communications blackouts. The turnover rate for IT staff in the banking industry, as another example, is 30–40% in some Indian cities where demand for talent far exceeds supply. Ninety percent of educated young people live outside hot-spot cities, and companies looking to build offshore operations are now focusing less on the narrow benefits of low wages and more on the overall strategic benefits of certain geographies.

"A company needs a process for articulating precisely what it needs from an offshore site, reviewing a variety of possible locations, assessing cost and risk," wrote Diana Farrell in "Smarter Offshoring," in the *Harvard Business Review*. The company needs to examine current and future conditions, including infrastructure and labor supply. "A process needs to be deeply rooted in the company's unique business needs, which may result in choosing offshore sites that aren't obvious."

All companies have similar initial reasons for considering offshore operations: to reduce costs, increase revenue, enter new markets, and employ new talent. But in industries in which the process of globalization has been going on for years and creating

CHOOSING AN OFFSHORE SITE

1. **Define** decision criteria.
2. **Collect** data.
3. **Weigh** criteria in proportion to company's needs.
4. **Rank** locations.
5. **Assess** dynamics of labor pool.

Consider these factors:
    Cost: current wages, infrastructure, real estate, corporate taxes. · Skill pool of labor. · Size of your particular offshore sector. · Presence of competing vendors. · **Environment:** government support and incentives and regulations, business culture, quality of life indexes, accessibility as in travel and airport. · **Market potential:** local and nearby markets, size and growth rates. · **Risk:** security (fraud, crime), regulatory (law, stability), economic (inflation, currency), intellectual property (data and IP protection). · **Infrastructure:** telecom, IT, real estate, transportation, power supply.

—From "Smarter Offshoring," by Diana Farrell,
Harvard Business Review, June 2006

new dynamics, companies need to do a lot more than just pick the latest hot-spot city. They need to compare the risks and benefits of certain sites as they relate to the company's business strategy.

This is where legal services is headed. The U.S. legal industry is moving beyond the first small step of outsourcing menial tasks to the next great leap of conceiving of a global marketplace in which to operate. The globalization of legal services will force providers to see beyond their borders, to rethink their business models, and to develop their entrepreneurial strategies in light of the global market of labor, services, information and technology.

Legal services will follow in the footsteps of financial services but at a faster pace. Once the governments of countries like India modify their laws to allow foreign-owned law firms, as they have for foreign-owned multinational corporations, firms will build offices overseas and employ local lawyers directly. *Bloomberg* reported in January 2009 that, despite long-standing resistance from the All India Bar Association, the Indian government was circulating a draft of new regulations for opening their legal market (see the interview with Rahul Matthan of Trilegal at the end of this chapter). And in February, the Indian government enacted the Limited Liability Partnership Act, Section 59 of which allows foreign law firms to establish a place of business—but not to practice law—in India. The stage is set. I predict the Indian legal market to open fully by 2012.

Legal providers would be wise to appreciate the trend of globalization, especially as it has played out in financial services, and take their first small steps into outsourcing as they plan their larger leaps into global entrepreneurship.

IT, BPO, and KPO

Companies outsource activities related to information technology, business administration, financial services, customer service, and more. A company contracts with a third-party provider, either in or outside the country, for the services. Outsourced IT activities include software-application management and development, data-center operations, testing and quality assurance, and more. Sixty-six percent of the companies on the *InformationWeek* 500 list of business-technology innovators say they outsource some IT offshore, up from 43% in 2004.

Business-process outsourcing (BPO) expanded from outsourced payroll services to include employee-benefits management, human resources, financial and administration processes, accounting, call centers, and other customer-service functions. Information technology makes this kind of outsourcing possible by harnessing the use of the internet, computer technology, and telecommunications systems. The phrase "information-technology-enabled services," or ITES, refers to BPOs that rely on information technology to facilitate their outsourcing relationships. About 80% of the world's financial institutions rely on outsourcers. Companies that provide BPO and IT outsourcing services include IBM, Wipro, Infosys, Accenture, Hewitt Associates, Capgemini, Genpact, and the Tata Consultancy Group.

Knowledge-process outsourcing (KPO) refers to activities that depend on workers with greater skill, education, and training. Data-entry activities are a common BPO activity. Outsourced activities in legal services, such as legal research and the drafting of legal documents, could be classified as KPO activities, because they depend on the training and talent (the "knowledge") of the person doing the work.

Infosys is emblematic of India's BPO potential. The $23 billion company based in Bangalore has 66,000 employees whose average age is twenty-seven. Like the other Indian IT companies Wipro and Tata Consultancy, Infosys is expanding its services from systems maintenance to software development, systems redesign, and consulting (expanding, that is, from business processes to knowledge processes). The starting salary for a software engineer in the U.S. is $60,000; in India, it is $5,000. The U.S. is the largest market for Indian outsourcers, and Infosys clients have included the U.S. financial-services firms of Aetna, Fidelity, ABN Amro, ING, American Express Bank, Bank of America, Citigroup, Goldman Sachs, and Visa.

Companies operate globally in very complex ways. They mix IT outsourcing with BPO offshoring and manage relationships between facilities and vendors in cities around the world. Continental Airlines uses an EDS center in India for software development and an EDS center in Brazil for finance. Accenture has woven a web of facilities spanning the U.S., Britain, Spain, Ireland, Canada, Philippines, India, China, and Eastern Europe. With this level of complexity, management has become critical to the success of the business. Nearly half of all U.S. bank offshoring operations save nearly 40%, according to Deloitte, but many run into trouble with sluggish performance over time. Companies are now holding their offshore providers more accountable for costs and outcomes by entering into shorter contracts (one year rather than three, for example) and by tying incentives to results.

U.S. companies insist on security and privacy controls that are stricter than some other countries provide as a matter of course. The Indian Information Technology Act of 2002 makes cybercrimes a federal offense, enforceable by India's Central Bureau of Investigation, but companies (especially banks and other financial institutions) insist that third-party vendors comply with even stricter security for customer data. U.S. financial firms require Indian outsourcers to comply with U.S. laws for privacy, confidentiality and security. Many outsourcers require biometric keys (a fingerprint scan, for example) for their employees. Employees rarely work from paper documents. They rely instead on computers where documents are stored on secure servers. Cellphones and cameras are prohibited in the offices. Other measures may include closed-circuit monitoring, dual firewall systems, and revolving passwords. Many outsourcing providers are certified for the internationally recognized BS779 and ISO17799 information-security controls.

Security at company offshore facilities, rather than third-party facilities, may be managed more directly. Companies with facilities in India, for example, include IBM, Cisco, Microsoft, and HP. With onsite management, they can more directly establish and closely maintain their own corporate culture to ensure data security and protected confidentiality.

When outsourcing to third parties, however, companies have two options. They can work hard to maintain the right corporate culture by collaborating with the outsourcer, as described above. Or they can rely on vendors to maintain vigilance on their behalf. These vendors vet outsourcers and manage the outsourcing relationships (and can more easily switch from underperforming outsourcers to other providers). The companies that provide this service are often called business-transformation outsourcers or BTOs. They manage the outsourcing and offshoring relationships as a service to companies looking to improve their business performance. This is the service that many intermediary companies are now providing for law firms and corporate clients who do not have the resources to oversee outsourcing companies on the other side of the globe.

The Transition to Legal-process Outsourcing

Law firms outsource, in or out of the country, many non-legal functions: their libraries, data processing, copying, financial and accounting services, and presentation-preparation services. The top 200 U.S. law firms are estimated to spend more than $20 billion a year for back-office work. So outsourcing promises significant savings.

But the shift from BPO to KPO (from outsourcing administrative and technical tasks to outsourcing knowledge-based, higher-value work) provides a road map for the shift of attention from outsourcing back-office support to outsourcing law-related activities (that is, the work of paralegals and associates). Legal-process outsourcing (LPO) can include document review, contract administration, patent applications,

> **"Law practice tends to follow business. Outsourcing is no exception."**
> —From "Flattening the World of Legal Services," by Mary C. Daly and Carole Silver, in the *Georgetown Journal of International Law*, Spring 2007

litigation support, legal research, drafting of pretrial motions and briefs, and more. One LPO company, Lexadigm, reported that it helped prepare briefs for submission to the U.S. Supreme Court and several Circuit Courts of Appeals.

In 2005, there were about twenty offshore LPO companies. Today there are over one hundred . . . and counting.

LPO outsourcers include Atlas Legal Research, Pangea3, Lexadigm, UnitedLex, QuisLex, Mindcrest, Evalueserve, and Manthan Services. These companies formed explicitly to provide outsourced legal services. OfficeTiger, by contrast, is a BPO company that has expanded to provide LPO. (Lumen Legal provides legal staffing solutions and has expanded to provide LPO services as a third-party intermediary, vetting and contracting with outsourcers in India, Israel, Sri Lanka, and elsewhere on behalf of corporate and law-firm clients.)

Polls published in 2009 support the growing trend of legal outsourcing as a strategy for corporate counsel. Legal OnRamp polled eighty-four in-house counsel from companies with $1 billion or more in annual revenue. Nearly half of the in-house counsel responded that 1–10% or more of their spending would be moved directly (or indirectly through outside counsel) to offshore providers by 2013. In a survey conducted by the UK Law Society, almost half

(25 out of 52 respondents) of the in-house counsel of major companies planned to move spending from law firms to other providers, with 40% of in-house counsel dissatisfied with traditional law-firm billing structures. And, as mentioned earlier, the Altman Weil survey of 115 general counsel found that 75% faced budget cuts for 2009; 53% planned to switch some work to cheaper outside counsel; and 50% planned to require more alternative fees.

Legal outsourcing takes three forms. First, U.S. companies may hire in-house lawyers and paralegals within offshore facilities (like GE's in-house legal department in India). Second, U.S. companies and law firms may handle the outsourcing themselves, contracting with LPO companies on a task or project basis. And third, U.S. third-party vendors may serve as intermediaries and facilitators between U.S. clients and overseas LPOs. With the opening of the Indian legal marketplace, law firms may be able to access directly the talent pool of Indian lawyers.

Outsourcing law-related tasks reduces costs. This is the initial motivation when companies and firms seek out legal-outsourcing companies. But the company or firm immediately realizes that choosing a vendor requires an evaluation process, one that accounts for expertise, experience, reputation, industry knowledge, flexibility, creativity, cultural fit, and more.

A few outsourcing companies could be fly-by-night operations taking advantage of the trend. Law firms and corporations, however, need to do more than weed out pretenders. Pretenders will not last long anyway, and dozens of legitimate and capable outsourcers will remain. (In fact, in 2007, a new trade association, the National Association of Legal Process Outsourcing Companies, held its first meeting in New Delhi. Thirty-three LPO companies formed the initial organization with the mission to promote the image of the Indian LPO industry. Over fifty companies have since joined.) More importantly, law firms and corporations need to find a good fit between their needs and the provider's capacities. They need to find reliable outsourcing partners capable of sharing their vision, performing at a high level, and supporting their business strategies.

Why India?

Legal outsourcing has taken off in many countries, including Israel, Australia, and Sri Lanka, but it has taken off in India on another scale entirely.

Indian law students may attend a three-year postgraduate program similar to the typical law-school experience in the U.S., or they may enroll in a five-year program that combines an undergraduate degree with a law degree. India has over 500 law schools. (For three decades, the Ford Foundation

THE GROWTH OF INDIAN LEGAL OUTSOURCING

"While most vendors start by offering lower value services and gradually move up the value chain by demonstrating domain skills and gaining client confidence, there are others who focus on specific high-end services or niches."
—Arun Jethmalani, CEO, ValueNotes

"High volume services like Document review, eDiscovery, Legal publishing as well as niche areas in Intellectual Property and Contract services will drive future growth in legal services offshoring."
—Neeraja Kandala, analyst and co-author of the July 2007 Study by ValueNotes

Summary Findings of the ValueNotes Study:
- India revenues from legal-service offshoring are estimated to grow from $146 million for 2006 to $640 million by the end of 2010.
- Indian legal offshoring employed 7,500 people in 2006.
- The number of LPO employees is expected to reach 32,000 by 2010.

donated millions of dollars to Indian legal education as part of a philanthropic effort to promote the rule of law around the world.) Every year adds another 40,000 law graduates to the pool of about six million attorneys. (Some estimates put the figure at 100,000 law graduates, but many graduates do not enter the labor pool; the supply of graduates exceeds available jobs.) The Indian legal system derives from British common law, and, as in the U.S., judicial decisions are based on tradition, custom and precedent.

Occasionally, Indian judges even cite American case law in their opinions. All legal education in India is taught in the English language. Starting salaries for Indian lawyers are 20–30% of the starting salaries for U.S. lawyers.

Industry analysts agree India will dominate the offshore-outsourcing industry (legal and otherwise) for the next several years due to a variety of factors, including government policy favorable to business (tax relief, exemptions from import/export duties, property-development subsidies, and infrastructure support) and the availability of a large and highly skilled labor pool. The largest democracy in the world, with a population of 1.2 billion, India is second only to the U.S. in its population of English-speaking professionals. Its middle class numbers 300 million and growing, and 350 million people speak English. Over 221 universities graduate over 3.3 million students every year.

Portrait of a City Racing toward the Future
The growth of Bangalore embodies the dramatic effects of globalization. Bangalore is the Silicon Valley of India. Major multinational corporations (like Microsoft, Texas Instruments, Philips, Novell, Synopsis, Hewlett-Packard and Motorola) occupy expansive office parks. Over 200 IT corporations have facilities there.

INDIA STATISTICS & INFORMATION

- Population: 1.2 billion
- World's largest democracy
- 350 million English speakers
- 22 official languages
- India is the world's youngest country with 50% of its people under the age of twenty-five.
- By 2015, there will be 550 million teenagers in India.
- 800 million people live on less than $2 per day.
- 40% of the world's poor live in India, including one-third of the world's malnourished children.
- India's IT industry has directly generated 1.3 million jobs, with 3 million indirectly created.
- 850 million live in rural areas.
- India has 17% of the world's population but only 4% of the world's fresh water.
- 53% of women and 30% of men are illiterate.
- Nearly 80 million cellphone users
- China recently surpassed the U.S. as India's biggest single-country trading partner.

Source: *Planet India* (2007), by Mira Kamdar

....

"Over and over, I have heard some version of the following radical strategy for India's success.... Bring the proven power of entrepreneurship to bear on the most intractable problems, but don't assume that private investment alone can do the job on the scale and speed required. Forge partnerships among business, government, and NGOs. Nurture networks and mentor relationships between those who have the know-how and those who want to learn; between those who have the capital and those who need seed money. Relentlessly drive down costs in order to drive down prices."

—Mira Kamdar, from the book *Planet India* (2007)

Bangalore has been flooded by waves of people looking for those jobs and hoping to improve their lives. The population has exploded. Over six million people live in the city, and about 350,000 live in the shanty towns scattered in the nooks of the ever-expanding metropolis. Tucked into the urban outskirts, these large interconnected networks of dwellings are supported by wood poles and sheltered by fabric the color of dust or sand. These shelters have been around India's highly populated urban areas for decades.

Bangalore sprawls like a morphing labyrinth. Observers worry that without a concerted, coherent response from government to improve housing, infrastructure, and utilities, Bangalore will suffer even as it enjoys its boom times. It is as if an economic revolution that cities of another era would have had decades to manage has erupted in Bangalore within the compressed span of a few years. This is not surprising, considering that the companies building headquarters and offices in Bangalore are mature multinational corporations. These companies can move in and build and launch operations within months, at a rate far exceeding the slow pace of the public sector. Local government is overwhelmed. In general, highways and residential complexes and airports take time to budget, time to design, and time to build.

"There has been a tremendous change in most cities that have grown as a direct result of software and outsourcing entrepreneurism," observes Rahul Matthan of Trilegal, which has offices in Mumbai, Bangalore, and New Delhi. "By and large the growth has been so rapid that the infrastructure in such cities has struggled to cope. Bangalore was not equipped to handle the sudden growth spurt, and its infrastructure has been severely affected. The government is still struggling to come up with sensible strategies to address these new developments."

While Bangalore sprawls, the city center remains the heart of commerce, entertainment, and shopping. The idea of the suburb, so familiar to Americans since the 1950s, is only just catching on. Most people prefer to live in the city, where the jobs are. The suburbs offer only limited opportunities for entertainment and recreation. However, the density of the urban area—the crush of traffic and people and buildings—drives increasing numbers to the outskirts. Electronics City, an industrial park in the southern outskirts, occupies 330 acres, and in the northeastern outskirts of the city is Whitefield, another technology park. The government wants to develop an IT corridor linking the two cities. The city hopes to introduce the metro-rail and move its interstate bus terminals to the outskirts of the city in an attempt to reduce congestion. Meanwhile, most development proceeds unchecked, without regard for zoning and planning. Private speculators develop at their discretion, building wherever they can as fast as they can.

Matthan confirms that the main impetus driving the entrepreneurial spirit in cities like Bangalore has been the economic liberalization that began in the 1990s. "As a result, Indian business suddenly has access to foreign capital. With the rapid improvement in telecommunications and information technology, entrepreneurs enjoy opportunities. New businesses have allowed even those sections of the society that might otherwise not have benefited from economic liberalization to find jobs and thus improve their status in life."

People continue to come to the city inspired by the many rags-to-riches stories publicized in the Bangalore media. The educated young people have a good sense of the big picture, and, as employees, they have an eye on the horizon. They are looking to work hard and move up.

The economic life of cities like Bangalore is virtually unrecognizable to the older generations. In the protectionist socialist economy of the recent past (pre-1990s), the secure paths to economic stability and social status were in the sciences, in professions like medicine and engineering. Careers in business were regarded as risky and limited. Today, recent graduates are scrambling to move to Bangalore and work in business: in technology, telecommunications, computers, software, and more, much of it in the outsourcing realm. Young people occasionally find that their parents resist or perhaps underappreciate their career goals, but as employees in this new economy, they earn sums of money that boost the finances of the household. Their new salaries also enable them to leave home, rent an apartment, and live in the cities with their friends and peers.

In service industries like financial, legal, and even medical, these employees will need higher education. Their career paths will depend on it. As the work product that legal-service vendors provide rises up the value chain, employees will supplement their education with sophisticated training. As much as the future of cities like Bangalore depends on foresight, design, and good planning, the careers of young employees will depend on education, training, and the desire to succeed. Given the current spirit of entrepreneurialism and the booming economy, the futures of Indian cities like Bangalore, Hyderabad, Chennai and Mumbai promise to be fascinating, raucous, a little wild, and endlessly surprising.

*"India has a huge need for law
firms, both to employ lawyers and
to serve clients.... But the main
point is that the legal market will
finally work in India the way it
works in other developed markets
around the world."*

RAHUL MATTHAN, *Partner*
TRILEGAL
BANGALORE, INDIA

INTERVIEW...

How has Trilegal evolved over the years?

We do legal work for clients as opposed to taking a project
for sourcing as do LPOs. In India, however, the line
between law firms and LPOs is blurring. At Trilegal,
we're at the high end of the legal services market, largely
because there are very few large Indian law firms.
Trilegal started in 2000, and today we're ranked the fifth
best law firm in the country, with the ranking based on
reputation, quality, and other factors. Today, we advise
primarily large international companies looking to
operate in India.

In what ways are the lines blurring between LPOs and Indian law firms?

The lines are blurring because increasingly LPO firms are
doing the kinds of work we're doing, like acquisitions.
In other words, they're going up the value chain from
low-level tasks to higher-level tasks, and they're

achieving due diligence at a higher level. When LPOs
started in India, people were doing claims processing
and other simple tasks that required only minimal legal
knowledge. Some LPOs headed by lawyers are now
moving up the value chain to provide more substantial
legal opinions. By law, they can't provide the final
opinion, but they are doing more work that supports and
refines the opinion.

Law firms like Trilegal tend to focus on India and India-
specific issues. We're qualified to practice Indian law.
LPOs tend to provide work to clients in the U.S., Europe,
and Australia, so they work with outside firms. That's the
sole difference. Increasingly, LPOs have people in their
system who are able to sign off on the final work. For
example, they might have U.S. lawyers heading up a team
of two hundred people who do work in India. Those U.S.
lawyers scan through opinions and sign off on them.

Do LPOs tend to specialize in either high-end or low-end work?

An LPO may start out doing high-end work, but they've
now realized that to keep the cash flowing they have to do
a mix of all kinds of work. So a hundred or two hundred
people perform low-level work that doesn't need sign-
off, and a smaller number will do work that requires
sign-off from U.S. lawyers. There is plenty of work in
litigation support, for example.

Will the Indian legal market ever open up to foreign firms?

I think that will happen in five years. In 2007 and 2008,
for various reasons, the government looked like it might
take a step in this direction. Nothing has happened
yet, but the background for it is falling into place.

We're getting new legislation. Many more people are now thinking along these lines. Given our election year in India and the economic crisis around the world, people are not focused on opening up the legal market right now. But in a matter of months, when our new government settles down, the pressure on the government to act will return.

What will be some of the consequences of the market opening up?
It will shake up Indian firms. Large UK law firms might come in and invest in training, all those good things, and then they will aggressively go after big Indian companies and the way they approach external legal services. Outside competition will increase the quality of legal services within the country, and it will also increase the consumption of legal services. In general, Indian corporates don't consume many legal services. They have small internal legal teams, but by and large Indian companies make many legal decisions without consulting their legal teams. These are decisions that U.S. companies wouldn't even consider doing without legal advice. Contract negotiations are still done by Indian corporate executives, without lawyers.

The immediate effect is that we'll have better qualified, better trained lawyers in India, who will be able to work in the same way that lawyers do around the developed world. Subsequently, that's going to have a knockout effect on LPOs. The effects are not all going to be good. It will cause some strain on the market. There will be a larger demand for good services and better opportunities for lawyers. It's possible that international law firms will provide better services to Indian businesses, but international firms will also hopefully recruit from the huge number of qualified and eager Indian law graduates and use these lawyers to service clients not just in India but around the world.

What is Trilegal doing in anticipation of this possible future competition from foreign firms?

We recently joined in a referral relationship with the UK law firm Allen & Overy, the third largest firm in the world. Our regulations don't allow for a merger. We are nonexclusive now. If both parties find the relationship valuable, we'll explore other possibilities if the Indian market opens. Other Indian firms are thinking along the same lines.

Are Indian firms laying the groundwork for future mergers?

When international law firms arrive, they'll either acquire Indian law firms to give them local presence, or they'll set up offices and cannibalize firms to get the best talent. There's a good chance that every firm and services provider will lose people. Indian lawyers will respond to the allure of working for a big international firm. Like any recent law graduate, young Indian lawyers will want solid, predictable careers with reputable firms. In India today, there are only around twenty law firms for a country of a billion people. There are plenty of lawyers, but only the top one percent perform any real legal work. The large majority perform low-level work. So India has a huge need for law firms, both to employ lawyers and to serve clients, such that if the legal market opens, it will still take a long while to fill the vacuum. But the main point is that the legal market will finally work in India the way it works in other developed markets around the world.

How will the open market affect LPOs?

LPOs will survive the opening of the market. International firms will not be coming to India to do LPO work. They'll come to establish a presence in the fastest moving economy in the world. Clients of LPOs wish they could set up in India, because there are only a handful of firms in India and only a few lawyers are any good. Local and international companies operating in India want more Indian firms to provide better services and higher quality work within the country. An open market will, however, put pressure on LPO recruiting. Qualified law graduates will rush to work for the big international firms. Then they'll go to Indian law firms. But even being third in line, LPOs will still have enough qualified law graduates to choose from. So LPOs may find it hard to recruit directly from top law schools, but that's probably a decade away.

What are the gender differences like among lawyers in India?

Our firm has a fifty/fifty ratio of men and women, although it varies across levels. This is true everywhere in the world. Once you get to the partnership level, very few firms have a fifty/fifty ratio. At the entry level, we have more women than men. The reasons have to do with the family, and it's an obstacle we're trying to solve. We don't have much daycare in India, but extended families are part of our culture.

In what ways are you using performance metrics?

In general, lawyers tend not to use metrics. It's hard for lawyers to incorporate business-school tenets into firms. The law is more about becoming an individual practitioner and less about working in a team. That's why it's different when we use metrics for lawyers.

We've found that metrics are good for analyzing firm
performance, measuring client satisfaction, and
providing employees with goals and feedback. People
want to know what's expected of them and how they're
meeting those expectations. Employees can see the five
steps necessary to reach a one-year target, and they
can track their progress. Employees want that clarity.
Otherwise, they're frustrated by arbitrary rules and
shifting targets.

We're going to implement a full-fledged system in a year.
Partners and associates are now in the training process.
We're working hard to build a meritocratic firm, and to
do that, there has to be some certainty about the manner
in which you grow the firm. Otherwise, it's based on
the whims of the people on top. That way has served
the Indian legal economy for a long time, but from our
perspective, it's not sustainable for the markets we're
going to face in the next few years.

What Are You Doing? What Should You Be Doing?

Business pressure can come from clients, namely corporate clients, demanding more for their dollar: more efficiency and productivity, especially at the level of basic tasks. General counsel may be the agents applying this pressure directly on firms. For their parts, general counsel are pressured by their client companies to cut costs and increase efficiency, just like every other department in the company. So they are doing what they can within their roles (such as reducing the number of firms they use for outside counsel, using contract staffing, and considering outsourcing both inside and outside the country) and insisting that firms do more of what they can (such as offer alternative pricing, eliminate premium pricing for basic tasks, and outsource non-law-related and some law-related tasks).

There are opportunities for achieving competitive advantages on many fronts. The 2009 Client Advisory released in January by Hildebrandt International and Citi Private Bank confirmed several industry trends and emphasized the urgency for law firms to employ new strategies in response to the recession. The report urged firms to base associate compensation on performance, alter the partnership-track system, reduce the number of partners, manage staffing more creatively and efficiently, experiment with alternative pricing customized for the project and the client, bring in project managers, and invest in business development and leadership training.

Law departments and law firms cannot do everything at once, of course. They compete in different markets and pursue different strategies. Change will take time and thoughtful planning. Unfortunately, the recession can induce a kind of panic and clutching at straws, which can be damaging in the long term. Now more than ever, lawyers need to consider their options and plan their strategies according to their own strengths and weaknesses. In many cases, firms are not accustomed to taking stock of their operations from the business perspective, at least to this degree. They might take stock in order to make minor adjustments, but today's pressures are forcing everyone to consider major shifts in strategy. Before they make any major change, however, both law departments and law firms need to understand their own operations and how they compare with their competitors. That brings us to performance metrics.

Good Data, Good Company

Before you think about what you should be doing, you need to know what you are doing. You need to collect data. Good companies know this.

Good business leaders know that to improve their company, they need transparency, accountability, and participation at all levels. They need information communicated constantly. They need individuals accountable for tracking and reporting information as well as for implementing tasks and strategies. They need the participation of all managers and employees in the work of the company, which means active and honest communication, ethical commitments to their work and co-workers, and the sharing of ideas for improvement and innovation. A strong positive corporate culture can foster the pursuit of these values. A fairly calibrated compensation system can provide proper incentives. A system for collecting performance data can support the business decisions that will keep the company competitive in the future.

All of this can go very wrong, of course. A compensation system that pits employees against each other can foster sabotage rather than cooperation. Without transparency (that is, without employees telling the managers what is really going on), employees can conceal bad news, unflattering data, and poor performance, and they will have an incentive to fudge the numbers if their own compensation depends solely on good news. (This is some of what was going on at Enron after Jeff Skilling replaced Richard Kinder as president of the company; Kinder had fostered a cooperative and transparent corporate culture while Skilling, his successor, fostered a selfish and deceptive one.)

When managers do not know what is going on in their own company, they are doomed to make bad decisions. They need accurate data to make good judgments. Employees, therefore, should not be punished for reporting accurate data, especially when the data represents bad news. Accurate information, whether bad or good, is exactly what managers need to know. Without accurate information, managers cannot make the changes that will allow the company to adapt and thrive in the market. Bad data kills companies.

Performance Metrics Moving into the Law

Over the years, companies have relied on a variety of models for collecting data and recording performance metrics within their organizations and comparatively with their competitors. Law firms, however, do not have a history of using performance metrics. They are not used to collecting data, communicating it openly, and encouraging transparency at all levels. The law as a profession has been guarded, resistant to change, and protective of its status as expert interpreters of the law and agents of justice.

For higher levels of legal practice, this mindset can be well justified. The practice of law can be an art that demands finesse, a sharp intellect, and a host of subjective skills developed over time through training and experience. Much of the practice of law does not require this level of attention. (This fact is why there exists an array of legal workers, from partners and associates to paralegals and law clerks.) Much of the practice of law is susceptible to standardization. The performance of low-level tasks can be measured. The first stage is to determine what data to collect and how to collect it using a standardized method.

There has been an attempt already to identify tasks according to a code system, and it is called the Uniform Task-based Billing Management System code (UTBMS). It arose out of an initiative in the 1990s among the American Bar Association, the American Corporate Counsel Association (now the Association of Corporate Counsel (ACC)), and a group of corporate clients and law firms. When a law firm sends a bill to a corporate client, the firm may identify in that bill each of the tasks by a code (composed of a letter and three-digit number). Currently, four sets of task codes cover the categories of Litigation, Bankruptcy, Counseling, and Project. In Litigation, for example, "Document/ File Management" is L140, and in Counseling, "Researching Law" is C200. When reviewing the legal bill, an in-house corporate counsel learns what tasks were performed, for how long (the hours billed), how much the task itself cost, and who performed the task.

This information represents a step toward greater transparency. Clients know more about what they are getting for their money. Theoretically, this information enables corporate counsel to compare law firms based on certain standard metrics.

Ideally, metrics can enable corporate counsel to make informed choices when they determine which outside firms can best handle certain legal services. Metrics can also enable corporate counsel to compare their own legal departments with the legal departments of their competitors. They can gauge relative performance by comparing the balances of in-house counsel with outside counsel and by the numbers of lawyers per quanta of revenue. Metrics also enable companies to assess the performance of their own legal departments, specifically by ensuring that tasks are assigned to the appropriate people, that low-value tasks are not being done at high-value rates, that work best done internally is not being contracted out, and that outside firms are not doing overlapping work according to different price structures. Data, in other words, brings transparency to the process, and transparency enables oversight. Oversight can then drive efficiency.

Few general counsel mandate that all law firms submit their bills using UTBMS codes. Both corporate counsel and law firms are still in the infancy stage of collecting, analyzing and utilizing performance data, whether using UTBMS or any other system. Why? There are several obstacles, all of which will be overcome. It is simply a matter of time.

First, the initial phase in which a system is created just takes a while. The legal industry has never collected performance data within firms or between firms. The practice of law has traditionally been regarded as too subjective to submit to objective methods of data collection. This is now changing. Corporations rely on methods of data collection and analysis, such as Six Sigma, and they are applying it to their legal departments. Without a tradition of data collection, law firms will be reacting to the systems of their corporate clients. (This was part of the impetus for the UTBMS codes in the first place, to kickstart a system with input from both lawyers and businesspeople.)

Second, corporations have often relied solely on corporate counsel (that is, on lawyers) to manage the analysis of the data. Lawyers certainly understand how best to manage legal matters in the interests of their corporate employers, but they are not trained in collecting and analyzing business metrics. If certain unique corporate counsel do understand (say, a person with a dual background in business and law), they might not have the time to devote to it or the incentive to make it a priority. Collecting data on the performance of law firms easily enough falls to the bottom of the to-do list. What will change this scenario are two quick fixes: a shift to different incentives and a shift to hiring people experienced in business analysis to work with the corporate counsel.

Third, the current generation of lawyers and corporate counsel are entrenched in habits (such as the billable hour and the partnership model), and the inertia of their roles and their circumstances has not yet been overcome. In other words, it is very hard for old dogs to learn new tricks. The old tricks seem to work just fine, the new tricks have not been clearly defined, and the rewards for these new tricks are rather abstract. While the circumstances are, indeed, changing, it is still conceivable that the entrenched generation (those who have committed decades of their lives to pursuing the billable hour and partnership equity) will not ever fully embrace the new way. This is very understandable and must be acknowledged. What it means, however, is that change in the industry will be driven by the next generations: by those junior partners who doubt the long-term survival of their firms, by those who might still be associates today, and by those now earning their dual law-business degrees. The next generation understands that the world has changed, that law firms cannot fulfill their promises if they do not adapt, and that entrepreneurship is a necessary part of the business of law.

Acceleration by Fire

In response to the recent economic crisis, many large law firms have laid off staff and attorneys by the hundreds. Even before the crisis, law firms endured high rates of attrition, associate turnover, and lateral moves by partners. Some of these talented people are bound to leave large firms completely and move to small and mid-sized firms. They might also start their own firms. The exodus of talent from the large, traditionally structured law firms may provide the perfect opportunity for the launch and development of newer, more flexible models. In other words, these attorneys can walk away from the fire and start over from scratch. They can assemble like-minded people and design, from the beginning, smaller companies with new missions and adaptive strategies. These budding firms can acknowledge the impact of all the industry trends and take the opportunity to envision new ways of managing legal resources. They can put in place flexible staffing, collaborative networks, project coordinators, performance metrics, systems of client and employee feedback, and more.

To Shrink and Predict

Corporate counsel will welcome these new firm models. Why? Because corporate counsel today have two initial objectives: to shrink their legal budgets and to make those budgets predictable over time.

Corporate law departments are trying to make the transition to a more predictable, manageable system. Performance metrics within law firms and law departments can be designed to do (at least) two things: to shrink the overall legal budget, and to reduce the wild fluctuations of legal costs year to year.

One of the biggest obstacles to achieving these objectives is the partnership model's reliance on billing by a premium hourly rate. The vast majority of legal expenditures is still based on hourly billables, and if the goals are to shrink the budget and to make costs more predictable, in-house and outside counsel have to start by rethinking hourly billing. They have to ask, "Can we make certain tasks more affordable by leveraging all the options of labor and technology now available to us?"

As a first step, corporate counsel want to find ways to shrink the budget immediately, perhaps by working with outside counsel or alternative providers that provide new staffing solutions for low-value, unbundled tasks. As a second step, and as a longer process that might take years (and involve long-term strategy, new relationships, and investment in technology), they want to find ways to make the expenditures more predictable.

Legal consultants, staffing companies, and other alternative providers are increasingly offering business consulting services to law firms and law departments. Today, the services most often include compensation and performance benchmarking for larger law firms and law departments that grapple with multiple international offices.

Soon, law firms and providers of all sizes will rely on consultants, staffing companies, and new, permanent legal managers to revise their business models. They will analyze their strengths and weaknesses by using performance metrics to assess what they are doing. Then, to determine what they should be doing, they will rely on the advice of outside consultants, in-house managers, and other legal resources to kickstart the design of sound business practices. Using performance metrics, feedback systems, and calibrated compensation models, they will shrink budgets, make costs predictable, and find ways to thrive in the new legal marketplace.

Interviews with Legal Visionaries

While the legal industry as a whole has been slow to change, the business of law has its share of leaders and legal visionaries. They are spearheading change, experimenting with new ways of doing business, and seeking innovation.

These interviews feature the timely perspectives of general counsel and law-firm partners who are responding directly to trends in the marketplace. Legal entrepreneurs and those from other legal-service providers describe how they are capitalizing on industry trends. And everyone discusses how they are planning for the future.

Interviews were conducted between September 2008 and January 2009. Final edits of the interviews were made in February 2009. This allowed interviewees to take into account the financial and economic turmoil of 2008–09.

26 · PAUL SMITH, PARTNER, EVERSHEDS
"We've been pioneers for over ten years now of alternative fees."

38 · DON LIU, CORPORATE SENIOR VICE PRESIDENT AND GENERAL COUNSEL, XEROX CORPORATION
"The trend to utilize data in the practice of law is stronger today. It's a good trend."

51 · DAN REED, CEO, UNITEDLEX
"What we've done is to say forget about law or business. Just break the work down to its essence and look at the whole organization."

65 · TYRONE FAHNER, PARTNER, MAYER BROWN
"We must staff efficiently if we are to make money as a law firm."

77 · ANONYMOUS, EDITOR, LAWSHUCKS.COM
"My goals are to present data in a useful fashion and to provide insider commentary on relevant stories."

100 · DEBORAH EPSTEIN HENRY, FOUNDER AND PRESIDENT, FLEX-TIME LAWYERS LLC
"The more we move work/life balance away from being a mother's issue, the more successful we will be in making change."

111 · CHRIS JOHNSON, DIRECTOR, GRADUATE PROGRAM IN CORPORATE LAW AND FINANCE, THOMAS M. COOLEY LAW SCHOOL
"If you don't increase the numbers of minority applicants getting into law school, then all the work I'm doing with firms is going to be limited by the flow of people coming out of law school."

166 · RAHUL MATTHAN, PARTNER, TRILEGAL
"Outside competition will increase the quality of legal services within the country, and it will also increase the consumption of legal services."

188 · JAMES POTTER, GENERAL COUNSEL, DEL MONTE FOODS
"We're going to see more people inside law departments who focus exclusively on process and efficiency and defining what value is."

193 · SUSAN FLOOK, GROUP GENERAL COUNSEL, THE BODY SHOP INTERNATIONAL
"When the firm sets up affiliations around the world, each affiliate has to be up to the same standards and have the same approach. They have to run the matter the way I want it run."

198 · ROSE BATTAGLIA, CHIEF OPERATING OFFICER, DEUTSCHE BANK
"The COO has become more of a strategic partner to the general counsel. We work together to become more effective and efficient in how we deal with our projects and outside counsel."

204 · GARY COHEN, GENERAL COUNSEL, THE FINISH LINE
"Some of my firms have taken our collaborative model and presented it to their other corporate clients. I want them to be successful."

207 · IVAN FONG, NOMINEE FOR GENERAL COUNSEL FOR THE U.S. DEPARTMENT OF HOMELAND SECURITY (DHS); FORMER CHIEF LEGAL OFFICER AND SECRETARY OF CARDINAL HEALTH
"I believe we are close to a tipping point back to a less adversarial, more value-driven model for legal services. The firms that respond to this call for change will thrive."

211 · DENNIS STRYKER, GENERAL COUNSEL, RICK ENGINEERING COMPANY
"Some places that supply lawyers for project-specific issues might become more important to some of us. New alternatives may change how we reach the talent pool."

216 · DAVID ROLL, SENIOR PARTNER, STEPTOE & JOHNSON; MANAGING DIRECTOR, LEX MUNDI PRO BONO FOUNDATION
"We may shed practice specialties as we move into premium areas, and I believe we will continue to selectively add laterals through aggressive lateral recruiting."

219 · PHILIP CROWLEY, ASSISTANT GENERAL COUNSEL, JOHNSON & JOHNSON
"When you create a business plan, act on it, and measure your progress with metrics, you send a message to your business clients that you share their paradigm, that your plans reflect their needs, and that you're holding yourselves accountable."

225 · DAVID PERLA, CO-CEO, PANGEA3
"This dual ability to pressure providers for new solutions and to employ new types of providers is part of a new trend."

230 · JOHN WALLBILLICH, CEO, LEXVISTA
"We favor consistent, smaller improvements rather than taking months (or years) to develop a more complex approach."

234 · RON GRUNER, PRESIDENT, THE VALLEX FUND
"The legal profession could benefit from outside investment, because in any industry new ideas often come from the outside."

"In the engagement of legal services, we must become better and more effective consumers. We're working to reconnect the cost of legal services with their value, and we're using processes, metrics and databases to achieve that goal."

JAMES POTTER, *General Counsel*
DEL MONTE FOODS
SAN FRANCISCO, CA

INTERVIEW...

How long have you been with Del Monte?

I've been general counsel at Del Monte for over seven years. Before Del Monte, I was chief legal officer for Prudential Direct, which included Prudential's retail-banking businesses. I represented banks and thrifts when we suffered through the savings and loan crisis in the 1980s. I learned from that experience that both increased regulation and deregulation present creative opportunities for lawyers.

How has globalization changed your role as general counsel?

It's now commonplace to talk about globalization and international business, but in terms of intensity and complexity of the law and legal culture, the U.S. continues to support one of the most developed environments. With respect to my role as general counsel, I am most involved in selection of foreign counsel. When we engage foreign counsel, for example in China or Thailand, Ecuador or Venezuela, we prefer to use local counsel. In fact, there are some countries— South Korea might be a good example—where you generally can't find branch offices of U.S. firms. If we can locate U.S.-trained lawyers in those countries, we believe that the common educational background is an overall plus. Regardless of whom we engage, we look to local counsel to explain the business and legal environments in which the company will operate. This becomes particularly important with respect to negotiating contracts and transactions, interacting with regulators, and managing FCPA compliance generally.

Have you tried outsourcing some work?

We have explored outsourcing—specifically to India—and encouraging our U.S. firms to outsource the review of documents in certain document-intensive litigation. We understand that some U.S. firms are reluctant to outsource because they want to maintain tight control over quality. We have found, however, that some legal-service providers in India will address that challenge by reviewing a certain amount of documentation at no charge, thereby allowing us to determine whether or not there is a quality difference between that review and the review provided by the resources of the U.S. firm.

How are you managing workflow to best coordinate your legal resources?

Del Monte, like most law departments, is moving toward a competitive-bidding process (RFP) for most key projects. Comparison shopping is one hallmark of a knowledgeable consumer, and in the engagement of legal services, we must become better and more effective consumers. So much of the historical engagement process was built on (and limited by) relationships. Selection criteria were not grounded in objective data, and the concept of value—a good job for a good price—was lost over time. We're working to reconnect the cost of legal services with their value, and we're using processes, metrics and databases to achieve that goal.

So, when it comes to managing outside counsel, we do that on a policy basis, employing a web-based matter-management and invoicing system to support our written outside-counsel policy. We also use annual evaluations to quantitatively assess an outside counsel's performance in several areas, including budgeting and cost. We couple that with a qualitative assessment of service and work product, among other things. As more and more law departments employ these types of tools, we will be able to share our experiences and become more knowledgeable consumers.

How has your relationship with outside counsel changed over time?

Over the course of my career, I've seen the relationship with outside counsel move back and forth from a partnership/collaborative model to one that is perhaps more project driven (which does not necessarily mean that it is not collaborative). Many practitioners believe that if outside counsel feels more like a partner with in-house counsel, then that relationship inspires outside counsel to be more engaged and effective. Those practitioners also tend to believe that competitive bidding on every project of significance is not conducive to building a long-term relationship.

My personal view is that relationships (without enforced metrics) tend to work against the client. Outside counsel tend to drift as relationships become more tenured and taken for granted. An outside firm with a long-standing relationship tends to lose sight of the fact that there are other firms competing hard for your business. It's the rare firm that continuously tries to provide its services more efficiently and volunteers ways to cut costs.

Now, some would argue that it is the client's responsibility to manage outside counsel rigorously and make sure the partnership continues to be mutually beneficial. The reality is, however, that drift occurs because most in-house counsel expect outside counsel to abide by the original bargain without day-to-day policing. And, once you allow outside counsel to drift, it's very tough to bring them back in line.

What are the biggest trends affecting you today?
There are two trends. The first is that the role of general counsel has become more difficult over the last five to ten years. The SEC, for example, is defining and redefining the function of a "gatekeeper," i.e., the person within the company relied upon by external constituencies to enforce laws and policies. There is, however, a bit of a disconnect between external expectations and internal practicalities, and the result is that in-house counsel must bridge the gap in a way that preserves internal relationships while maintaining external trust.

The second broad trend is the increasing pressure on in-house counsel to select and manage outside counsel in a fashion that obtains the greatest value for the client. Some of my remarks above address this trend.

How will the role of corporate counsel change in the next decade?

Legal departments need a clearer idea of how to add value to the company's efforts. By that I mean not only what the company recognizes as value, but also what thought leaders would recognize as value. I've been amazed by the data that dramatically shows the differences between what lawyers do and what clients value, as well as between what clients value and what's most effective in managing risk and exposure and controlling costs.

Law departments are twenty years out of touch with best-in-class processes. Consequently, our clients will increasingly insist that business consultants be brought in to analyze the internal processes of the legal department. These consultants can create a blueprint, but you have to have the resources inside to understand it and execute against it. Few law departments include people with the necessary business and process skills to analyze how the department should best conduct its function. Over time, we're going to see more people inside law departments who focus exclusively on process and efficiency and defining what value is.

How do you think you will leverage information technology in the future?

Information technology will commoditize much of the practice of law. Questions will be answered, contracts will be constructed, and discovery will be conducted online. Social networks will put the best thinking of thousands of attorneys at every practitioner's fingertips. Knowledge management and delivery will be one of the law department's highest functions.

"Outside counsel have got to substantially change the way they charge for and deliver legal services.... The basic fee-earning structure in law firms is wrong. The whole thing needs a sea change."

SUSAN FLOOK, *Group General Counsel*
THE BODY SHOP INTERNATIONAL
LONDON, UK

INTERVIEW..

How will the role of corporate counsel change in the next decade?

Corporate counsel are becoming more like business partners than strict academic advisors on the law. Recently that went a little too far in the U.S., and so the overreaction after Enron was that the role of in-house counsel was pulled back to more of a compliance-officer role, to being a guardian of the corporation, ensuring that it complies with the laws of the land every which way. I wonder where that's going to go.

Twenty years ago, in-house legal counsel were regarded as naysayers and policemen, and businesspeople tended to regard them as necessary evils and pushed them away from business decisions. Then over time the businesspeople found counsel could be useful if they sat in and listened to strategy at an executive level. They found that their general counsel could identify danger areas early, so the company didn't go down the wrong road in the first place. That was found to be very valuable. Good in-house counsel can help the company achieve its objectives without running afoul of the law. General counsel have more on their shoulders these days in terms of compliance and looking at what the business is doing to ensure they don't go off the rails. I don't know where that's going to be in ten years. In my view it will be sad if the general-counsel role goes back to just compliance/regulatory responsibility and less involvement in business decisions, because they can do both and add a great deal of value.

What changes should outside counsel be making to help in-house counsel respond to their budget pressures?

In my view outside counsel have got to substantially change the way they charge for and deliver legal services. It is my opinion that the basic fee-earning structure in law firms is wrong. The whole thing needs a sea change. In my dealings with outside counsel and pushing for change in the way they bill us and the way they work for us, I'm just one person chipping away at this, but increasingly my in-house colleagues are thinking along the same lines. In my view there are big changes coming to law firms and the way they approach fees. The true value of advice given will become a serious consideration and the concept of the hourly rate will go.

How can law firms change when they're getting a variety of abstract demands from multiple clients?

Firm structure will change as a result of dialogue between general counsel and outside counsel. If the in-house community can get together and explain what is wanted, and we all ask for similar things, law firms will realize they will have to change to provide the service their

clients require. More companies are putting in place
in-house legal counsel. In the past, the company had to
accept the law firm's advice and billing rate because they
didn't know better, but now they want to have expertise
on the inside. Premium pricing from law firms has
grown exponentially without people giving thought to
what alternatives could look like.

How do you let outside counsel know what you're after?
I don't want to pay a law firm for delivering an academic
   tome when all I need is good commercially focused
   advice having regard to the relevant legal considerations.
   We want to know the legal difficulties involved in going
   down path A or B. We don't want an exhaustive survey of
   case law. If you work with one firm over time, they get to
   know you and what you require.

**What do you do as a board member of the Association of
   Corporate Counsel?**
As a member of the International Committee of the board,
   I have responsibilities for expanding its international
   presence. The organization is based in Washington, D.C.,
   and it promotes the role of in-house legal counsel and
   the in-house profession generally. Its reach is global,
   although its main presence at this time is in the U.S.,
   Canada, and Europe, with some tinkering around the
   edges in Asia. There is growing opportunity to expand
   into Asia. India, for one example, is a fast-growing
   country for business opportunities. We are looking to see
   whether or not the Indian in-house profession would
   be interested in the ACC establishing a presence there.
   Good, gutsy law firms are there. They are local, but they
   have international affiliations. India will have a thriving
   legal in-house community eventually.

Will law firms adapt to globalization by consolidating and specializing?

This is a much discussed subject. The little guys will focus on local businesses. And there's a strong role for boutique firms servicing clients within their countries. The bigger law firms are spreading their tentacles around the world to provide clients with international service.

How do you pressure the larger, global firms to be responsive to your needs?

If I have a project and more than one country is involved, I prefer to have a law firm that I know has high standards. When the firm sets up affiliations around the world, each affiliate has to be up to the same standards and have the same approach. They have to run the matter the way I want it run. They all have to bill me the same way. I don't want to keep explaining who I am or what I want or educate them about my company's business. The London firm has to explain all that to their affiliates. So I am one who goes for the law firm with multi-local presences. It doesn't mean I'll stay with them in every location. In some locations they may not have the expertise, or they may fail to provide the service required. I've moved away from local affiliates of a major law firm when the service was not to the required standard. Then they get on the phone asking me why, and I tell them. I think it is helpful to explain to the firm why you are leaving them. And I don't go back until I know the problem I encountered has been fixed.

Have outside law firms rolled out the fixes you inspired to their other corporate clients?

My law firm appointed a global client auditor who goes around asking its clients what's wrong with the firm and their affiliates. That person feeds the information back into the firm's management committee. They distill the constructive criticism from clients and make changes to the firm globally. It's a completely new role for a senior person who becomes a client-care partner. They travel the globe, checking out offices, and speaking to clients about constructive criticism. They're not just looking at themselves. They're looking for perspective from outsiders. I think that's fabulous.

What is the future of the partnership model for law firms?

Some different way of doing business will evolve for law firms. I am not sure what impact that will have on the current partnership model. Change will come because somebody's brave and shows the way.

"Those law firms that have better processes for managing workflow ... will be able to rise above the firms resistant to change. These firms will be able to offer a more competitive price and not need to compromise quality."

ROSE BATTAGLIA, *Chief Operating Officer of Legal Department*
DEUTSCHE BANK
NEW YORK, NY

INTERVIEW...

What do you do as Chief Operating Officer (COO)?

My role as COO in the legal department at Deutsche Bank is similar to the role of an executive director in a law firm. I'm involved in budgeting, hiring, cost management, technology planning, and department strategy. I support the general counsel, and the department supports the business and senior executive committee of the Bank. The lawyers do the legal thinking, and my team gives them the tools to do what they do best.

If you think about the amount of legal and regulatory change going on globally, it's impossible for one general counsel to know it all; he relies on his regional general counsels and the senior partners at our preferred law firms. So having a structured legal department to support him is critical.

How long have you been the COO?

I've been the global COO for the legal department
here since 2003. Prior to that, I was the global chief
administrative officer at another investment bank. And
from 1992 to 1999, I was at an international law firm
supporting the global head of litigation.

What's changed in your COO role?

The role of COO has become more prominent in the legal
department. The trend started in 1999. Since then,
the COO has become more of a strategic partner to the
general counsel. We work together to become more
effective and efficient in how we deal with our projects
and outside counsel.

At Credit Suisse, I was the chief administrative officer, and
my focus was on ensuring we had the right technology,
the right head count, followed the cost policies, and
could report our law-firm spending. We were looking
at how we charged the business. Like a law firm, we
charge our clients, except internally. We were the service
provider to the business in an investment bank. At that
time, number crunching was more critical than thinking
about strategic partnership. We weren't thinking about
streamlining. We were figuring out how much we cost,
since law departments were growing, almost to the size
of mid-size law firms.

The shift came from market pressure. The business
also became more sophisticated, and they realized
they needed more legal support. We created more
documentation teams to address drafting and
negotiation. Paralegals were doing more analytics. Legal
departments kept growing, adding more non-lawyer
staff to support the larger number of lawyers. Ten years

ago, the legal departments of investment banks were half
the size and mostly lawyers. Now some banks have over
800 people, with forty percent non-lawyer staff.

How has the recent financial crisis affected you and your legal department?

The volume of business has gone down. Price has become
key. We're doing more competitive tendering. That's
never happened before. There was a time it was viewed
as an insult to call and ask a law-firm partner if they
could provide a quote for the services prior to seeing the
invoice for time and materials. It's no longer an insult.
It's become common. If there's more than one firm
that can do the work, we request a quote from each. We
then look for the best quote and hold them to it. They
can't just throw us a low number to get the deal and then
deliver a higher bill.

Law firms have responded, "If you get a better quote,
call us back," because they don't know the right quote.
This is a symptom of the failure of an industry to
change. Those law firms that have better processes for
managing workflow and have standardized templates
for documents, for example, will be able to rise above
the firms resistant to change. These firms will be able
to offer a more competitive price and not need to
compromise quality. And this creates opportunities
for all firms, not just the big firms. They also need to
start offshoring and nearshoring. They need to find
creative ways to use their resources more efficiently and
effectively.

How have you been improving the efficiency of certain legal functions?

In the last five years, we've entered a world of process improvement for legal departments. Teams of project managers have been hired to look at current process. In the heat of litigation, while cases like Enron and WorldCom were taking place, there was so much documentation to review that neither in-house departments nor law firms could handle it with their current staff. Document reviews were being handled by third parties, and not by firm associates but by temporary staff to save costs. The quality was all over the place. So I became a price junkie with temps. Companies in India were hiring people with a more strategic vision. They hired smart lawyers, trained them on discovery, and even trained them on our own process of document review. We were able to easily see quality and could review the work ourselves through the extensive MIS (Management Information System) they produced.

We went down the road with a few pilot programs, and now we have a robust process within Deutsche Bank. If you want to outsource a function, you need the right operating procedures and documentation. And now, two years later, we have all our major document reviews done offshore. Even lawyers on smaller reviews prefer to use offshore vendors. In many cases, we do this in conjunction with our outside law firms. The law firms do a quality review on top of what the vendor does. So outsourcing is controlled by the law firm and us, the client. The cost is less, the turnaround is quicker, and the work product is of high quality.

How are you using performance metrics to evaluate your vendors?

We work with offshore vendors that already have metrics in place for our review. In our own offshore locations, we've tweaked those metrics. You want metrics to pick up errors, but you also want to measure the completion rate of tasks and projects. We're separating matters into categories. For example, we separate the documents that can be delivered quickly and without much negotiations from those that will need to be heavily negotiated. Then we can measure what we've done in the past against what we're doing now.

As legal departments evolve, what kind of people are needed to staff them?

We still need excellent lawyers, but we need project-management skills from inside and outside the legal industry to complement the lawyers. For recruiting, we now look at people from accounting and consulting firms for those project-management jobs. We find people with good project-management skills and put them with people with good legal understanding, and we get streamlined, top quality, cost-effective processes.

Are you evaluating law firms differently?

It's still about relationships, but there's a process now. It's not enough to have a good lawyer. You need to make sure the firm is innovative. You look at reputation, the quality of lawyers, the profits per partner, associate pay, associate turnover, diversity, but that's not enough. We want to meet the people running the firm, and when they come out to negotiate rates, we don't just want the senior partner who's been around for thirty years. They are expected to understand more about Six Sigma and technology and process improvement. They need to sell their firm and its innovative processes, not just a partner and his reputation. In meetings, more outside counsel are now telling us about offshoring, their use of technology, and the better ways our legal department can interact and share knowledge with their firm. These innovators will be recognized going forward and will continue to receive accolades and more business.

How should legal education adapt to changes in the industry?
A couple of law programs have approached us. They're not ready to convert classrooms, but an introduction will start to happen in law schools. Law students and young lawyers will start taking internships with legal departments like ours and see the way we think and operate.

"Partners are breaking away from big firms and creating boutique shops. I use these lawyers for their expertise. I get the same value and better service for less cost."

GARY COHEN, *General Counsel*
THE FINISH LINE
INDIANAPOLIS, IN

INTERVIEW..

What does your company do?

The Finish Line sells athletic shoes. We have seven hundred stores in forty-seven states. We also sell apparel at ninety-five Man Alive stores in twenty states. I've been general counsel since July 1997. Before that, I was a senior partner at the law firm of Cohen and Morelock in Indiana.

How do you find your outside counsel?

I rely on referrals from other general counsel. If they tell me a firm is good, that's the best referral I get. But I'm always looking for somebody with a new way to get it done. Good performance doesn't mean we need a successful result. I just need to feel they've gone through the appropriate processes. Being outside counsel as long as I was, I understand their world. I'm at the table with my outside counsel, and the good ones appreciate it. I'm hands-on. I encourage the young attorneys. Now that

I've set up our model and protocol, I'm trying to pass that on. My goal is to have my processes and knowledge stay here at the company.

What trends do you see impacting the law-firm model?

Partners are breaking away from big firms and creating boutique shops. I use these lawyers for their expertise. I get the same value and better service for less cost. The Law Department Consortium Marketplace is all about collaborating. Its website and services help connect in-house counsel with outside counsel. You might find one or two partners at a big firm who get it, then they have to go up to management to say we have to rethink our model. They might try it out on a beta basis. And that's why boutique firms will do better. They'll start at six lawyers and build to thirty, but they'll only bring those who are up to speed with the new model.

What are you doing to move from the hourly rate to alternative fee arrangements?

I've tried several things. We might pay the hourly rate up to a certain point in litigation, and from then on switch to a flat fee. I might add premium incentives for time-sensitive matters. I might pay sixty percent of a bill and figure out the balance at resolution. One Seattle firm adds a line on the invoice for me to add or subtract. If I'm dissatisfied with the firm, I'll write in a deduction. If I'm happy, I'll add something. It's a feedback tool, and they can gauge my dissatisfaction. To me that was a good value proposition. That was a firm looking for communication.

Are you using software to help track billing and performance?

Through the Law Department Consortium, we have software to communicate with key firms. Our in-house staff can break down the data to make sure we pay only so much for certain tasks. As long as the quality is there, it's win/win for us and outside counsel, if they're smart. It pushes them to become more efficient. You watch for trust in these arrangements. You look to see if they're cutting corners to still try and make it in the old model, or if they're really improving things.

How have firms reacted to your push for change?

Some of my firms have taken our collaborative model and presented it to their other corporate clients. So I've helped them build their firm business. I want them to be successful, and I'll promote firms who collaborate well.

I knew I was doing it right when a major firm asked me to lecture new associates on how to approach me as a corporate client and how not to approach me. Older partners came in and listened too. I'm inclined to help partners in larger firms. The biggest mistake on their part is to assume in-house counsel are corporate drones. We know the other side at law firms. So we know when we're being billed for template pleadings. We know what firms are doing to pad hours. Once you break my trust, I've got firms behind doors two and three, and they're dying for my business. If you play games with billable hours, I won't be nasty. I just won't open your door again for new business.

The smart firm leaders know this and are taking their time. It's not client cultivation now. It's maintenance. You have to maintain trust and good relationships with clients. Every in-house counsel is looking for something to make them look good in the eyes of corporate officers. As general counsel, we have a lot of pressure on us to maneuver through corporate waters and provide legal knowledge. If outside counsel make me look good, I won't forget it.

"I believe we are starting to see fundamental changes to the way legal services are provided.... Corporate clients are becoming increasingly sophisticated and, with good data, can drive their law firms to be more efficient."

IVAN FONG, *Nominee for General Counsel*
FOR THE U.S. DEPARTMENT OF HOMELAND SECURITY; *Former Chief Legal Officer and Secretary,* CARDINAL HEALTH, INC.

INTERVIEW...

What trends are impacting the legal industry?

I would say that the biggest trend is ever-increasing cost pressure, leading to a greater focus on value and results. Indeed, I believe we are starting to see fundamental changes to the way legal services are provided. For example, we are seeing more and more matters being handled through alternative fee arrangements, such as flat fees, capped fees, success fees, or contingency fees. These fee structures align the law firm's incentives with those of a client to complete a project efficiently and successfully. It allows the law firm to share some of the risks of an unsuccessful result as well as the benefits of a successful result. In most other areas of economic activity, service providers price their services based on value and results, rather than time spent. Corporate clients are becoming increasingly sophisticated and, with good data, can drive their law firms to be more efficient.

Another trend is the increasing use of technology. In our intellectual-property practice group, for example, our outside firms use online software tools to manage and keep track of our patent prosecutions. We can store and share documents in a way that provides instant access to those who need them. Over time, I envision law firms providing global access to their work product to clients who pay a fixed fee for access to content.

There is also the increasing global nature of modern large corporations, which means that law departments must manage people and resources across international boundaries and time zones. When I first came to Cardinal Health, we did not have lawyers outside the U.S., even though the company had a growing international presence. U.S.-based lawyers did the international work, and that made no sense to me. So we moved those positions to Europe and Asia, and we hired lawyers who had in-country expertise and were locally qualified. That's where the clients are. And you want a situation where businesspeople walk down the hall or pick up the phone in the same time zone to talk to their lawyers. As a result, service is more efficient and of better quality.

How do you see law firms changing in the next decade?
I see law firms focusing more on providing value, rather than simply billing more hours at higher hourly rates. The traditional business model of law firms provides little or no incentive to provide services more efficiently. When law firms start measuring and competing against other firms on value, that is when we know we will have succeeded. If a niche firm or small firm can provide the same or better quality of service than a large law firm at a lower cost, then those firms will get more work.

How do you see the relationship between in-house counsel and law firms changing over time?

I see the relationship between in-house counsel and law firms changing in fundamental ways. Way back when, law firms acted as trusted counselors to businesspeople. CEOs had direct relationships with senior partners in law firms, which had longstanding relationships with their large corporate clients. An invoice would be the classic one-pager, one line, for "services rendered," and a number. And there was enough trust that it worked.

Beginning a few decades ago, a stronger in-house bar assumed the role of trusted counselor. I and others were attracted to in-house positions because we could be closer to the business and their most significant legal, business, and strategic matters. Firms became legal service providers, a step removed as trusted counselors. At the same time, transparency to law-firm economics meant that law firms began focusing more on "Profits Per Partner" rather than value and results for clients. This led to a dynamic of greater in-house control over outside counsel, more scrutiny and auditing of law-firm invoices, ever-increasing billable-hour requirements and billing rates, and "free agency" among law-firm rainmakers. The result is an unhealthy, sometimes adversarial relationship between in-house lawyers, who are under severe pressure to drive efficiency and productivity, and outside counsel, who are (rightly or wrongly) perceived as being under pressure to maximize revenue for the firm.

This brings us to where we are today, where I believe we are close to a tipping point back to a less adversarial, more value-driven model for outsourced legal services.

The problem is not the $1,000-per-hour senior partner, who often adds significant value, but the army of $450-per-hour junior associates who are doing document review. In-house counsel are quickly realizing that the basic economic model of most law firms does not serve the interests of their corporate clients. They are now demanding change, and the firms that respond to this call for change will survive, be profitable, and thrive.

How do you move toward a more cooperative relationship?

I'm involved with a project of the Association of Corporate Counsel called the ACC Value Challenge. It's an effort to transform the way we think about the provision of legal services. It focuses on the concept of value and reconnecting the cost of legal services to the value provided. We first need to figure out how to measure and then pay for value. For firms, this may mean fixed fees for projects or stages of projects, leaner staffing, better mentoring, more focus on client service and results, and the like. For in-house lawyers, this may mean going back to longer-term, trusted relationships, giving firms greater continuity of work, and better communication of expectations and budgets. For both sides, it will mean greater collaboration, dialogue, and professional satisfaction.

"We have been looking at other methods for controlling costs. I've been striving more and more to break down tasks to find the cost value."

DENNIS STRYKER, *General Counsel*
RICK ENGINEERING COMPANY
SAN DIEGO, CA

INTERVIEW...

Are you using performance metrics in any way?
We're looking at metrics internally, and we're looking
at how our internal clients are performing, and how
we're providing the information necessary to the legal
department so it can perform its function. We haven't
applied metrics to our external firms in a formal sense.
Informally, we've been looking at bottlenecks and
readjusting some of those things. We've been looking at
how we store, retrieve, and maintain data, so I can look
at what they've done for us without them sending over
reams of paper. We also look at the documents we're
providing them. Our litigation is typically over a project
or construction issue. Our files are massive. And you
really don't want to spend a whole lot of time with law
clerks or associates or outside legal-service staff and run
through this stuff for hours. A lot is electronic, and we
can figure it out relatively quickly.

Have you tried competitive bidding?

I've thought about but have not moved toward bidding, in part because our company doesn't do much bidding, and we want to be philosophically consistent. We have been looking at other methods for controlling costs. I've been striving more and more to break down tasks to find the cost value. There has always been reluctance to doing this over the years, so it's been a slow process. When I was in private practice, almost all corporate and securities transaction work I performed was done according to a flat fee or a value fee, determined regardless of hours. We asked, "What value did we add? Why come to us in the first place?" In transactions, it's become easier to get law firms to understand this concept. Litigation, however, is still a difficult area to work with.

How difficult is it to try something new in the workflow process?

The problem is you may end up with piecemeal stuff when firms aren't ready to make broader decisions. We've slowly gotten our litigation people to understand how things are done and to start working to improve efficiency. For example, not all the firms had yet thought about using extranets and other ways to share documents. Google Docs is not perfect because it's unsecured, but it's a model to look at. We were looking at a space in the city, and the law firm used by the developer was smaller. So we used Google Docs to work on the lease simultaneously. I'm not that worried that the world might figure out how much rent we're paying. So that worked out okay for us. You couldn't use unsecured file-sharing in litigation, of course. We have our own secure FTP site. To see even a particular item in a particular folder, you need passwords. It's one way to streamline when some law firms aren't ready to make bigger leaps.

What's it like being a general counsel today?

I speak with friends from large organizations, and we talk
a lot about management expectations. It's not what it
was years ago. It's not a nine-to-five job. I had to be in
Phoenix recently, and in the airport lobby, I'm on the
phone with two other offices. I use the Blackberry on the
plane as long as they let you. There are not enough hours
in the day.

Our company has grown over twenty years. The amount
of work has grown, too, but the staff doesn't grow
proportionally with that. Contracts are also more
complicated today than they were even five years ago,
and yet the time frame has shortened to complete all
these tasks. We sent something to a group in Chicago
on a Friday afternoon. First thing on Monday morning,
their lawyers had emailed it back, and by that afternoon,
they were asking if we'd made a decision yet.

**What do you see as the expectations of the next
generation?**

I haven't figured out yet whether the next generation has
such different expectations than we did, or whether we
have our own filters and tend to make distinctions bigger
than they are. Some say the current generation expects
to be in charge right away. I think that view is a bit
jaded. I think the current generation expects to work on
meaningful things. Sitting around reviewing depositions
for six months is not meaningful. You stick it out for the
experience, but then you go somewhere else to try and do
more meaningful work.

When a first-year associate enters a firm, they probably
assume that it is not the place where they're going
to become partner. But in some respects, we in the

previous generation had already learned that. Most of us did not develop our careers at the same place we started, in part because we weren't sure what we wanted to do. The current generation experiments more with what's out there to find out what resonates with them before settling on a final career. They believe they've got time on their side to figure it out.

How do you see the role of corporate counsel changing in the next decade?
In the next two to three years, I'll be doing exactly what you were asking me about. What are we doing about metrics? How can we talk to firms to persuade them to change their methods and become more efficient? There's always this short-term mentality about what any change does to the business this year versus what happens years from now. In the short run, I'll have to convince law firms to rethink, to consider hiring an outside consultant to come in and analyze what they're doing and then figure out ways to improve what they're doing.

The overall provision of law services is going to change in five to ten years. I'm not concerned about whether or not to offshore, but I am concerned about having the right talent at a reasonable rate of return and having the work done at a timely pace. Since I began practicing, everyone's been saying law firms are changing, but they might finally be changing, and they might end up not looking the way they have in the past. Some places that supply lawyers for project-specific issues might become more important to some of us. We may be turning to them more. New alternatives may change how we reach the talent pool.

We're a small corporation, and five years ago, we didn't
do international work. Now we do. For us to look at a
property and the surrounding area in Costa Rica is not
that hard anymore. Google has made it easier to track
that information down. If you subscribe to Google
Earth, you have so much information available. Sitting
at desktops, we're now doing work where we weren't
working before. I don't know lawyers down there, but I
need to find people. Through networks like Lex Mundi
and the Association of Corporate Counsel, you can find
referrals. Even small companies work around the world.
Even the small firm where I used to work consolidated,
merged, and got bigger.

I see myself in a role where you need to have a much
broader view of what the practice of law is. We're small,
but we can see thousands of miles away. It used to be
difficult. Now it's not.

"There is pressure on rates, but really the pressure is for efficiency."

DAVID ROLL, *Senior Partner*
STEPTOE & JOHNSON; *Managing Director*, LEX
MUNDI PRO BONO FOUNDATION
WASHINGTON, D.C.

INTERVIEW...

What do you do?

I wear two hats. I'm a senior partner at Steptoe & Johnson,
a Washington, D.C., law firm of about 500 lawyers, and I
run an international *pro bono* legal-service organization,
which draws upon a network of 160 law firms throughout
the world to provide legal advice to social entrepreneurs.

What trends do you see your law firm following?

The firm is heavily oriented to litigation, federal
regulation, tax, international trade and IP law. Our
firm will continue to seek a balance, probably sixty to
seventy percent devoted to litigation and various forms
of dispute resolution and the remainder in transactions
and other non-contentious matters. Having a good
balance helps during bad economic times, when
litigation remains strong. I see firms like ours increasing
the differential in profitability between the top-tier law
firms and the rest of the firms in the *AmLaw* 100.

I don't see us doing much legal outsourcing. We will
continue to increase our efficiency in litigation by
sourcing our document-review work through an in-
house document-review center, in a building outside
D.C., employing hundreds of people. I may be overly
optimistic about how we're going to survive in the
coming years, given what's happened recently, but I
think we're as well positioned as any *AmLaw* 100 firm to
maintain if not increase our profitability, which has been
on an upswing the last ten years.

We may shed practice specialties as we move into premium
areas, and I believe we will continue to selectively add
laterals through aggressive lateral recruiting. I see us
being in China in the next two years. We have offices in
Phoenix, Chicago, New York and downtown L.A. and
Century City, and we're already in London and Brussels.
I don't see us merging with anyone. I see us continuing
to acquire individuals or groups with substantial proven
books of business in high-end practices which add
or relate to our existing signature practices. We were
successful in attracting a national bankruptcy lawyer
in anticipation of what's going on now. Restructuring
should be a growth area. Our government relations group
in D.C. will be extremely involved in the next few years,
with legislation that will cascade off of the subprime
crisis and the worldwide financial downturn.

**What kind of pressure is there to change your billing
practices?**
There is always pressure from general counsel at client
companies. There is pressure on rates, but really the
pressure is for efficiency. We have so far been successful
in attracting the kind of business where the stakes are so
high that the hourly rate is not as important as the quality

and efficiency of the lawyers doing the work and the risks the company is trying to manage. Another area is international trade where whole industries are at stake. An industry can virtually disappear if it is sanctioned for engaging in dumping or unfair trade practices or is the target of those practices, and so then you have an industry willing to pay for the best lawyers in that specialty. That's our world, but our world could change.

What about bidding out some of the work?
I was involved in an organization in 2000 to 2002 that attempted to convince general counsels at *Fortune 500* companies of the wisdom of competitive bidding by major firms for substantial chunks of legal work. There was much talk at that time about how competition among top-tier law firms could drive down costs, and it has persisted. While I was involved, the organization successfully engaged in getting major firms to bid against each other to secure portfolios of legal work, mostly litigation. After I left, the organization has continued to operate, although it has not achieved scale, and it has not made much progress in reducing the legal costs of major corporations. Through competitive bidding, corporate legal departments can achieve savings, but it's a risk that many general counsel are not willing to take, because the low bidder may not end up being the best. Still, if you take a hundred cases of a certain kind, say, asbestos cases, you ought to be able to put some kind of price on them.

"A number of larger firms are in trouble, and I view the root cause to be the unworkability of the current paradigm over the long term."

PHILIP CROWLEY, *Assistant General Counsel*
JOHNSON & JOHNSON
NEW BRUNSWICK, NJ

INTERVIEW..

How long have you been at Johnson & Johnson?

I've been in the law department at Johnson & Johnson for twenty-six years and am currently responsible for online training compliance, which I established here in 1999. Before 1999, I spent two-thirds of my time doing mergers and acquisitions and a third doing FDA-regulatory work for our high-technology medical products companies. I serve as U.S. Environmental Law Counsel, and I've been serving on the board of the Association of Corporate Counsel (ACC) since 2007.

What do you think of performance metrics and business plans?

I'm in favor of them. If you take a process apart and analyze it, it's frequently possible to streamline the process and then automate it. Reasonable metrics permit you to measure improvements in productivity. The most successful automation projects have been preceded by mapping the existing process, re-engineering the process, and then automating that re-engineered process. There is a great deal of focus on metrics these days. I spoke at an ACC meeting in Seattle about creating business plans for law departments. Many lawyers feel they can't put together a strategic plan, because their responsibility is to react to the legal risks presented to the company, and it's impossible to predict what those will be.

Developing a business plan creates an opportunity to sit down with your colleagues on the business side and identify risks. You can discuss what they're most worried about in terms of growing the business. A legal business plan can be a useful resource-allocation tool. You could do any one of a hundred things right now, and there's no guarantee that tasks selected at random would have the overall effect you want for the business. Having a strategic plan changes that. A strategic plan helps you identify which goals to focus on. At the end of the year, if you have an appropriate metric, you can measure what you did and how much progress you made.

The challenge is to create the plan in a thoughtful way with plenty of client input. When you create a business plan, act on it, and measure your progress with metrics, you send a message to your business clients that you share their paradigm, that your plans reflect their needs, and that you're holding yourselves accountable. It's one thing to say something, and another thing to back up your words with actions.

What is the relationship of the law department to the rest of the company?

The best law departments have always been intimately involved in the business they support. The tradition of our law department since its founding in 1934, with Ken Perry, was based on a commitment to understand and participate in the business and be a partner. This is not to say we don't enforce limits. But after we tell them they can't follow a particular course, it's part of our job to help them find a legal method of achieving their goals that is also consistent with Our Credo. Our Credo is the one-page statement of principles that has guided Johnson & Johnson since its initial publication in 1943.

The prior general counsel, Robert Fine, used to tell candidates during their interviews that at Johnson & Johnson we don't hire lawyers to practice law; we hire lawyers to drive our business in a legal and ethical manner. So the idea is for our lawyers to use their legal skills to find ways to help the business create value. That helps our lawyers to be seen as valuable business partners rather than impediments.

In what ways do you communicate with the business side?

We talk informally about services and whether or not they need more support. This kind of communication resulted in our law department growing from seventy lawyers in 1996 to over 280 lawyers today. That growth was a reaction to the demand from business leaders for more help in many areas. Communication is part of the planning process, even though it might occur informally early on and in a more structured way later. It's a very important part of helping business partners appreciate the value of what we do and thereby commit resources to a larger, more collaborative legal function.

We also want to better understand the drivers of client operations and find ways to limit risks and liabilities and capitalize on opportunities. We're in the pharmaceutical

and medical industries, which are heavily regulated.
Lawyers who understand their client's business are in
a better position to capitalize on the legal regimes in
place or that could be put in place with the appropriate
influencing of state or federal legislatures.

**How has globalization affected Johnson & Johnson and
its law department?**

In the twenty-six years since 1982, Johnson & Johnson
increased its worldwide sales from about $5 billion to
over $60 billion and doubled its employees from 60,000
to 120,000. The law department went from forty lawyers
in one office location to over 280 lawyers in forty-one
offices around the world, including in Europe, China,
Japan, Singapore, and India.

**How does the law department manage the workflow
around the world?**

Our response is driven by how we're staffed. In the
U.S., we handle some litigation internally, but even
litigation handled by outside counsel is closely overseen
by our lawyers. Our ideal is to have a knowledgeable
internal lawyer intimately involved with the cases and
actively involved in shaping strategy, particularly in
methodology, as well as in the assessment and review of
budgets. We want to keep a close eye on what the case is
costing us and what it might cost over a period of time.
In Europe and Asia, we have fewer lawyers, so we have to
rely more on outside counsel. But we also have much less
litigation there.

**How do you see the size of law firms changing in the next
decade?**

On the question of whether or not law firms will grow
bigger, I'm agnostic. A number of larger firms are in

trouble, and I view the root cause to be the unworkability of the current paradigm over the long term. If you're a Skadden Arps or Cravath Swaine & Moore or Sullivan & Cromwell at the top of the food chain, you can have that paradigm. Other firms need to rethink the process by which they create value for their clients and enter into discussions with clients to make that work. The ACC Value Challenge (see www.acc.com) has advanced discussion and understanding by the outside-counsel community (as well as in-house counsel) of the costs built into the current system. We've seen quite a few firms work with ACC and our members to address the issues of law-firm structure, practices and costs.

Why is the paradigm unworkable?

Here's just one example. Many firms will bring in large numbers of first-year associates, because they realize that fifty percent of them will leave the firm in two years. Wouldn't it be better to hire fewer associates and create an environment to encourage them to remain? The associates punch their tickets and leave, and this high turnover results in costly retraining, not to mention client frustration. So how do you do this? That's a good discussion to have, and that's what the ACC is focused on. Accountants, architects and other professionals find ways to price engagements for doing something and create value their clients want. The last holdouts are lawyers.

How will the role of general counsel change in the near future?

It will become more proactive and more focused on planned reduction of risks. For example, we developed an enhanced approach to compliance training. We visited with over 6,000 senior leaders over the course of about four years in an attempt to be more proactive. We wanted to help them identify the areas of risk in their businesses and learn to ask for help from us to plan and work around them. In a sense, we wanted our law department to become less like a group of firefighters running to put out the next fire and more like collaborators with our businesspeople to be the designers and builders of fireproof buildings. It's an application of process re-engineering. You attempt to design the opportunity for error out of the business process to the maximum extent possible. The result may not be perfect, but it is generally a great improvement on the process it replaced. After the process has been set, we encourage continuous improvement, refinement, and efforts to help people remain vigilant to the risks they face.

"I think many legal departments today are no longer following the old approach. They don't get rewarded for not taking some risks. There is more risk-taking today, more embracing of innovation."

DAVID PERLA, *Co-CEO*
PANGEA3 LLC
NEW YORK, NY

INTERVIEW...

What is Pangea3?

We are one of the leading providers of outsourced legal
services from India to large global legal departments and
large global law firms.

When did you start Pangea3?

Pangea3 was founded by Sanjay Kamlani and me in the
summer of 2004, and we opened the doors of Pangea3 in
India in the beginning of 2005.

How has the work of Pangea3 changed?

There are more players like us now, and that demonstrates
the growing acceptance of this as a real career choice
for Indian attorneys. High-caliber candidates apply to
work for Pangea3. We don't have to explain what we do
anymore, like we had to when we first started this. In the
beginning, it was really novel. So everyone who joined
had to be an innovator. But now young lawyers in India

know us. They know what we do. And in the U.S., the understanding of our business is vastly higher. Most legal departments know what kind of work we do. We don't have to devote hours to justifying our business model or explaining why they're talking to us. It's a hugely different business today.

How many large, serious legal-service vendors are there in India now?

There are over one hundred legal-outsourcing providers, although out of that number only five or six are really good. Maybe another ten have been around a while. Then there are lots of boiler rooms. They may have no American lawyer at all, or maybe only one who goes back and forth from India to the U.S. trying to drum up business.

What trends in legal services do you see?

There's a trend toward holding legal departments to cost metrics in a way that other departments have historically been held to. Managing the costs of legal departments is not new. What's new is the notion that a legal department should be subject to the same metrics that you subject other departments to. That's a major trend. It's more than mere pressure. There are measurements and metrics.

Another new trend is that legal departments today are much more willing to experiment and be wrong in order to find something new and innovative and right. I think many legal departments today are no longer following the old approach. They don't get rewarded for not taking some risks. There is more risk-taking today, more embracing of innovation.

Where is the pressure to innovate coming from?
I think the pressure is coming from the executive level
at corporations. The trend is coming internally, and
as result of feeling this pressure from within their
companies, general counsel are saying, "I'll look to
legal-outsourcing companies, consultants, innovative
domestic companies, even software companies and
new software. I'll look at nearshoring or best-shoring."
They're open to looking at everything. They're reacting
to being pushed and being told, "Look, we're not going
to hold it against you if it doesn't work. We're going to
give you latitude as an in-house lawyer to make some
mistakes."

Now, they can't be wrong on strategic legal advice, but they
are getting more leeway when it comes to searching for
innovative ways to provide legal counsel. Companies are
pressuring law firms for global pricing, unitized pricing,
banded pricing—all sorts of alternatives to the usual
tactic of just discounting the billable rate. Some of these
work and some don't. It depends on the circumstances.
But companies are pushing firms to try something new.

As a contrast, back in 2001 when I was general counsel at
Monster.com, at the subsidiary level, the order was given
that everyone should go to the top providers (and I went
to all the big law firms) and tell them to cut their rates by
ten percent. And that was all we did.

Today, if I were in that position, I would look at a host
of different solutions: outsourcing, offshoring,
nearshoring, other types of providers and organizations
like virtual law firms. I would go to a law firm and say,
"Forget the billable rate. I want you to start unitizing. I'll
give you a certain number of contracts and litigation, but

you have to unitize it. You have to bear some risk. But I'm not paying by the hour."

This dual ability to pressure providers for new solutions and to employ new types of providers is part of a new trend.

What are some examples of this at Pangea3?
We came to a conclusion with one of our clients with whom we do nondisclosure agreements to have a fixed rate per nondisclosure agreement for that client, not a monthly retainer. This provides our client with cost certainty. They can stay within their budget because they know the exact price they will be charged per agreement. With other clients, we have full-time equivalent engagement, so they own a team of people based on a rate over the course of the month. You don't get money back for going under, and there's a window if you go over a little.

How hard is it for a law firm to change in response to general counsel pressuring them for alternatives?
Firms are usually not able to move as a single entity. Some firms move more like corporations, but most firms do not. A corporation is a dictatorship, a CEO makes decisions, and there's a mission. A law firm is not a dictatorship. Firms are run by committees. There are practice groups. And they react to clients in different groups. That means law firms are much less flexible. There is very little imposed as a corporate decision.

We've worked with law firms, but that only means a partner was told by one of his or her clients that the firm needed to work with us. At a corporation, they all know who you are when you work with them. Your name gets shared. Information is shared. But at law firms, there are often many individual fiefdoms, if you will, and everything is a case of first impression.

I think what general counsel are now trying to do is to wake up their own outside counsel to the shortcomings of this dynamic. The challenge is the general counsel may only be able to influence the partner that serves their business, but not their entire firm. So to pressure for alternatives, the general counsel has to trust that the partner can move the firm. If a client company is big enough, firms will listen.

Because of the complexity of alternatives available today, a new trend in this area is that larger law departments have chief administrative officers or operating officers who are lawyers, and their roles are to look at innovative solutions. The first step is to decide to have someone look at this. The second step is to centralize the process under someone who reports to the general counsel. Some major companies have people in this new role now.

How do you see the size of law firms changing in the next decade?
I see the trend of consolidation continuing. There will be small or big firms, but it will be hard to be in the middle. The only firms trying to stay midsized are the ones trying to do something differently. They're offering regional distinctions or specializing. But there's a size at which it's not sustainable. The cost structure is too much to bear, and the margins aren't compelling enough. I started my legal career with Rosenman & Colin, and that firm merged after I left in 1999. Today, it's Katten Muchin Rosenman, and it's more than doubled, maybe tripled in size.

"We favor consistent, smaller improvements rather than taking months (or years) to develop a more complex approach."

JOHN WALLBILLICH, *CEO*
LEXVISTA
ANN ARBOR, MI

INTERVIEW...

What is Lexvista?

Lexvista is a legal advisory and development firm based in Ann Arbor, Michigan. We work on a consulting basis with general counsel and corporate legal departments to improve corporate legal performance. We also develop and deploy online resources for corporate counsel. One of our new initiatives is Planet GC, which will provide general counsel with management tools on the desktop starting in the first quarter of 2009 (and located at www.generalcounsel.net).

Do you consider yourself a legal entrepreneur?

I guess the market will ultimately be the judge of that. I have launched a few legal-related ventures: a weblog for general counsel, the Wired GC, in 2004, and Lexvista LLC in 2006. I think the challenge for any legal entrepreneur is balancing knowledge of the law in the modern enterprise with required business strategies.

The good news is that I was a general counsel for twelve years and an in-house lawyer for five years before that. That helped in knowing where to begin and focusing on bringing value to the market. But turning ideas into a viable business is something I have to work at every day.

How is the role of general counsel changing?
General counsel today have to deal with issues of complexity, cost, and communication on a global scale. Historically, general counsel could focus on legal services. As companies have grown and as the law has become more complex, general counsel are now legal executives with broad management responsibility. In those roles, they oversee larger expenditures, with growing internal staff and increasingly expensive outside counsel. So while general counsel are more ingrained in the fabric of the business today than ever before, they are drawing more attention from the CEO, CFO and the board of directors. Fortunately, there is also more communication among general counsel today through professional organizations, business networks, and online resources (like Legal OnRamp and hopefully Planet GC).

What's your take on the use of performance metrics?
The legal departments of larger companies have been subjected to metrics that are used throughout their operations to improve performance. Because of the slowing global economy and increased competition, smaller law departments are also becoming more performance-oriented. Any general counsel knows that most law firms bill by the hour and make more money by raising rates, working longer, or assigning more people to the project. We help general counsel take a fresh look at their outside spending and department operations.

We favor consistent, smaller improvements rather than taking months (or years) to develop a more complex approach. We want our clients to move ahead on their own.

Do outside counsel respond differently than general counsel to the idea of alternative billing?

I'm focused on general counsel, but I do some work with law firms. And some firms are trying to price services according to value or a budget. But general counsel have to drive the process, starting with asking firms for new ideas that embed savings and incentives for improvement. If the firm won't do this, the general counsel will have to find another firm that will. Law firms need to hear a consistent message that change is not just a passing fad. The undercurrents of change have been building for many years. What I'm seeing in my work with general counsel is that even the biggest firms are paying attention now. Will they continue to when the market improves? The jury's out on that.

Do you recommend offshoring as a strategy?

Legal matters don't always need to be done by lawyers. For low-value or repetitive work, you can use a strategy that couples offshore or lower-cost resources. General counsel need to manage workflow with and without lawyers, using technology, and exploring other resources.

What are some of the first steps you advise people to take?

I discourage people from trying to reengineer their whole legal department on the fly in a short period of time. Start with some big-cost items. For example, pick your top five firms according to their annual billing, and look at what they're doing for you and compare their performance with other firms. Talk to other in-house counsel. For repetitive work or work similar in scope, try to improve the efficiency, maybe by pricing it on a monthly basis. Fix one thing at a time, then go to something else next quarter. Some general counsel experiment with RFPs, which can become very complex and time-consuming. These days, how do you know that the firm you select in your RFP this quarter will still be around next quarter?

What are you hoping to provide to general counsel with your new venture, Planet GC?
General counsel have unique responsibilities in the C-level suite. They may be expert in certain areas of substantive law, but they quickly learn that many of their challenges involve business issues. Planet GC will provide an information filter to general counsel, as well as management tips and tools in a convenient desktop format. We'll be adding features as we grow.

"Every complex business eventually realizes that projects need two bosses, a creative expert and a project manager. These are two separate skills, and few can do both, especially at the same time. The legal profession hasn't yet realized this."

RON GRUNER, *President*
THE VALLEX FUND
ANDOVER, MA

INTERVIEW..

What is The Vallex Fund?
The Vallex Fund (vallexfund.com) is focused exclusively on encouraging entrepreneurship in the process, as opposed to the practice, of law.

What is your background?
My background is business. I don't have a law degree. I have been involved in various aspects of the law, particularly litigation for thirty-five years as a plaintiff, witness, expert and defendant. So I definitely have views on how law in the U.S. is practiced from the perspective of the client.

What motivated you to encourage entrepreneurship in the law?
After I sold my company, Shareholder.com, a few years ago, I began to think about issues in the business of law that frustrated clients. If you do a Google search,

you'll find hundreds of articles dating back at least
to the 1970s about abuses and inefficiencies in the
discovery process, as well as many articles on the abuses
of hourly billing. So it occurred to me that within itself
the profession is very conscious of these issues, but
there has been very little change. Consequently, there's
a huge amount of pent-up frustration. So it struck me
that one of the catalysts for change might be to encourage
entrepreneurship.

What are the opportunities for improving billing?
Most general counsel can't give you a detailed analysis of
the typical costs for discovery, depositions, pleadings
and other matters. So systems that could identify and
categorize costs across geographies and industries
would make billing less opaque and provide general
counsel with better means to understand their costs and
negotiate fees.

**Is the unbundling of legal functions into tasks part of
what can make improvements possible?**
We believe there is an opportunity for entrepreneurial
firms to help manage the administrative aspects of
lawsuits using project managers and skilled specialists,
the way movies are made or buildings are built. They
would work for the general counsel in a company
involved in litigation. The team could use traditional
project and vendor management and tools to organize
and manage the administrative aspects of the case.
These kinds of tools are used successfully in other highly
complex projects. Law is not different. Much of what
runs up litigation costs are outside experts, witnesses,
and document review, and all those things can be
unbundled and sent out to bid.

In my experience with major lawsuits, I've found that inevitably the lawsuit's lead attorney, rather than a separate manager, is managing the entire lawsuit. It's like having the brain surgeon manage the nursing staff and stock the operating room. Every complex business eventually realizes that projects need two bosses, a creative expert and a project manager. These are two separate skills, and few can do both, especially at the same time. The legal profession hasn't yet realized this.

What other opportunities are there for entrepreneurs to improve the legal system?
Most everyone agrees that the U.S. system of zealous advocacy is a good system, but it's expensive, especially when the law covers certain high-knowledge areas like medicine, pharmaceuticals, and computer technology. Experts on both sides are paid high fees to advocate opposing opinions. In the middle is an over-worked judge with likely no background in that particular technology or specialty. In other jurisdictions of the world, judges are supported by the court's experts.

I provide an example of how much experts can differ in my case study *Anatomy of a Lawsuit*, which I posted on our website. My company sued a competitor who, we claimed, had hacked into our company's computers. Critical evidence, of course, would have included any emails between the defendant and our clients that might have involved our proprietary information. The defendants' expert claimed it would cost $35 million to provide these emails. Our expert claimed that it would cost only $140,000, and we even offered to pay for searching the emails. We fought the defendants for two years, and yet the issue was never resolved. If the judge had had access to a competent, independent expert, perhaps the court could have resolved this matter quickly and efficiently. That would certainly have been the case in a normal business transaction. So the system can be improved not by changing the law but by improving the process of law.

What is The Vallex Fund doing today?
We're hardly a year old, so we're still involved with educational activities. We launched the website, which provides several white papers, and we're working with Lexvista on a series of seminars covering changes in the legal profession. The audience is mainly corporate general counsel. The series is available through Lexvista's WiredGC.com. We're also, of course, looking for entrepreneurs who can build companies.

What will The Vallex Fund be doing in five years?
Ideally, we will have invested in a handful of companies developing constructive ways to improve the process of law. We'd like to be involved with a small number of companies (financing, organizing, or running them selectively) that improve the accountability, transparency and productivity of the practice of law in the U.S.

How do you find entrepreneurs in the legal field?
We've been surprised. In high-tech, the industry I come from, there's no lack of entrepreneurs. People come out of school and want to start companies right away, like Google and Yahoo were formed. In the legal profession, if someone is an entrepreneur, they tend to be sole proprietors practicing law the way they want to. We're seeking people who want to run a company, not practice law. It takes time to locate these people.

Is it also a matter of finding investors?

That's certainly more of an issue now than it was a year ago. But it's not a critical success factor. The legal profession could benefit from outside investment, because in any industry new ideas often come from the outside. The legal profession has grown internally for over 200 years, financed by its own fees, which means there is no outside capital or outside thinking in the profession. So it could be healthy, although given the last few months and what's happened to the investment-banking system, it's not without risks. Outside investors could help the legal industry to think differently and innovate, but this would be detrimental if the pressure is only for short-term profits as we've unfortunately seen in so many other sectors here in the U.S. recently.

Conclusion

What will the legal industry be like in twenty years?

I imagine my daughter Sarah in 2029 watching a documentary made in 2019 about what changed after the economic crisis that shook the world in 2009. This is like what my family and I did back at Yellowstone Park. In 2008, we watched a 1998 documentary about a 1988 fire. Looking around at that time, we could not have guessed that a fire had devastated the park, or that the vibrant park that surrounded us in 2008 was the result of twenty years of renewal. The legal industry will be like this. The next ten years will see dramatic change, major recovery, and the total transformation from a profession to a business. It will be noted as remarkable. And ten years after that, in 2029, my daughter will be amazed to hear about the 2009 crisis—*"What was that all about?"*—and the transformation that took place in the aftermath.

The fire still burns here in 2009. But it is clear that the companies and law firms flourishing in the landscape ten years from now will be either entirely new providers or else existing law firms that totally re-invented themselves. They will start from scratch with new visions, and they will build new business models designed to achieve those visions.

What has to happen in the meantime? People inside the legal industry must start thinking like entrepreneurs. This has to happen first. The industry has to open itself not just to change, not just to enduring a rough patch, but to the earnest examination of how legal services can be provided better, faster, and cheaper. This is how entrepreneurs seek out business opportunity. They ask how something can be done better, faster and cheaper. This kind of thinking must start inside the industry before entrepreneurs outside the industry can participate.

The legal industry is the best industry for today's entrepreneurs. The legal industry has been ripe for change for a long time. Its traditions have persisted long past the time when similar traditions in other industries have been challenged, abandoned, and replaced. For this reason, entrepreneurs have a wealth of opportunities in the legal industry. Legal information and resources will be more widely available to clients and consumers. Networks will enable professionals to share information, work product, and access to clients. Providers will assemble teams of people from all over the world who can connect digitally and collaborate efficiently. These improvements will benefit companies, clients, consumers, and legal professionals. As the industry changes in response to these innovations, the entrepreneurs who invested their money, time and creative vision will see immediate and long-lasting returns.

For decades, the legal industry has made incremental advances. There has been experimentation with alternative fees. Staffing has become more flexible; complementing full-time staff are temporary, contract, and flex-time workers. Law firms outsourced back-office administrative and technological work, and now they are outsourcing law-related work using best-shoring strategies for combining local, regional, and global resources. But now unprecedented economic forces have cracked open the industry. Yes, change has been incremental in the past. No longer. The industry has been shaken at its foundations. To survive, those inside and outside the industry must work together to develop wholly new ways of providing legal services.

There will be a new breed of creative professional unbound from the billable hour. Today's professionals may be highly compensated, but that is changing. Many are unhappy with sacrificing their personal lives to rack up thousands of billable hours a year, especially now that the crumbling partnership model can no longer guarantee partnership as reward for those years of sacrifice. The economic crisis is forcing change upon the industry, but discontent will drive change from within it. Entrepreneurial professionals will create places to work as exciting as any in Silicon Valley. The legal market must open up to allow that sort of participation. Insiders must shape the perception of the legal industry sufficiently for entrepreneurs to see the opportunities. Without the industry changing in this way, the best and brightest entrepreneurs and attorneys may choose not to stay in the industry. They may choose not to enter it in the first place.

Lawyers who understand the trends and recognize the changes being wrought upon the industry have a chance. But if risk-averse lawyers hesitate, sit back to review more data, and wait to see what happens, this procrastination will allow others to claim space in the market, and to pull ahead. The longer you wait, the farther—and faster—you will have to go just to catch up. You will be left behind in the ashes.

The soil will soon be fertile. Entrepreneurs inside and outside the industry will see opportunity, plant their seeds, and work to survive and thrive in the legal marketplace. In time, innovation will rise up. All of us have to start to work today to be part of that new growth. But if you choose to wait and see, don't worry. You can always visit us in the future—as a tourist.

List of Graphs & Charts

Resources

Articles

Abraham, Thomas Kutty. "India Lawyers Should Stop Opposing Foreign Firms, Bhardwaj Says," *Bloomberg*, January 23, 2009.

Adams, Edward A. "What A Legal Recession Looks Like," *The ABA Journal*, January 2009.

Armour, Stephanie. "Generation Y: They've Arrived at Work with a New Attitude," *USA Today*, November 8, 2005.

Basu, Subhajit. "Offshore Outsourcing: How Safe is Your Data Abroad?" *Global Jurist Topics*, September 9, 2006.

Baxter, Brian. "U.S. Legal Job Market Contracts in 2008, Says Government Report," *The AmLaw Daily*, January 9, 2009.

Belkin, Lisa. "Who's Cuddly Now? Law Firms," the *New York Times*, January 24, 2008.

Bellman, Eric and Nathan Koppel. "Legal Services Enter Outsourcing Domain," *The Wall Street Journal*, September 28, 2005.

Binham, Caroline. "Linklaters Will Cut 120 Lawyers Due to Credit Crisis," *Bloomberg*, January 29, 2009.

Breitman, Rachel. "Lawyers, Pros Say Flex Schedule's Time Has Come," *The American Lawyer*, July 21, 2008.

Brook, Daniel. "Made in India: Are Your Lawyers in New York or New Delhi?" *Legal Affairs*, May/June 2005.

Brown, David T. "Middle-Market Firms Thrive Among Giants," *New Jersey Law Journal*, Vol. 189, No. 5, July 2007.

Buhai, Sande L. "Act Like a Lawyer, Be Judged Like a Lawyer: The Standard of Care for the Unlicensed Practice of Law," *Utah Law Review* 87, 2007.

Carlile, Nathan. "An Urge to Merge?" *Legal Times*, Vol. 30, No. 27, July 2, 2007.

Cima, Greg. "Legal Aid Online," *Pantagraph*, July 14, 2007.

Colman, Heather. "Collaboration Through Wikis at Hicks Morley," LLRX.com, January 29, 2009.

Constable, Marianne. "The Shuffle of Things: Law and Knowledge in Modern Society," *Theoretical Inquiries in Law*, January 2007.

Cotts, Cynthia. "India Wins Rising Share of Legal Work from U.S.," *International Herald Tribune*, August 22, 2007.

Creswell, Julie. "Law Firms Are Starting to Adopt Outsourcing," the *New York Times*, October 27, 2006.

Daly, Mary C. "Flattening the World of Legal Services? The Ethical and Liability Minefields of Offshoring Legal and Law-related Services," *Georgetown Journal of International Law*, Spring 2007.

Davey, Mark. "Outsourcing Strategies: Catering for a Refined Palate," *The Banker*, December 1, 2006.

Deshpande, Swati. "Foreign Law Firms Can Register in India, Says Law Minister," *The Times of India*, January 24, 2009.

Donde, Ritwik. "RSM Plans to Enter U.S. Corporate Taxation Space," *Economic Times* (India), October 11, 2007.

Editors. "Shanghai, Dubai, or Bye-bye? Prestigious Firms Face Layoffs, Collapse, and Other Indignities," *The Economist*, November 27, 2008.

Engardio, Pete. "Let's Offshore the Lawyers: DuPont is Farming Out Legal Services to Asia—and Saving a Bundle," *Businessweek*, September 18, 2006.

Farrell, Diana. "Smarter Offshoring," *Harvard Business Review*, June 2006.

Ferguson, Tim. "Gen Y is Setting the Tech Agenda," *Businessweek*, July 30, 2008.

Fried, Jennifer. "Outsourcing Reaches Corporate Counsel," *The Recorder*, August 25, 2004.

Galanter, Mark S. and William D. Henderson. "The Change Agenda," *The American Lawyer*, December 1, 2008.

Glater, Jonathan D. "Billable Hours Giving Ground at Law Firms," *New York Times*, January 29, 2009.

Goldberg, Elizabeth. "Exit Strategy," *The American Lawyer*, August 1, 2006.

Goldhaber, Michael D. "Global Law Firms Rule (Or Maybe They Don't)," *The AmLaw Daily*, November 24, 2008.

Guy, Sandra. "Outsourcing the Lawyers: Mindcrest Sends *Fortune* 500 Companies' Repetitive Tasks to Attorneys in India," *Chicago Sun Times*, June 6, 2007.

Healey, Jack. "65,000 Jobs Are Cut by U.S. and Foreign Companies," the *New York Times*, January 26, 2009.

Heilman, Dan. "Sharply Focused Practices," *Finance and Commerce Daily Newspaper*, November 17, 2007.

Henderson, William D. "An Empirical Study of Single-tier Versus Two-tier Partnerships in the *AmLaw* 200," *North Carolina Law Review*, June 2006.

Henry, Deborah Epstein. "Facing the FACTS: Introducing Work/Life Choices for All Firm Lawyers Within the Billable Hour Model," *Diversity & the Bar,* November/December 2007.

Henry, Deborah Epstein. "The Case for Flex-time and Part-time Lawyering," *The Pennsylvania Lawyer,* January/February 2001.

Hierschbiel, Helen. "How to Avoid the Land Mines of Discrete Task Representation: the Ethics of Unbundling," *Oregon State Bar Bulletin,* July 2007.

Irish, Charles R. "Reflections on the Evolution of Law and Legal Education in China and Vietnam," *Wisconsin International Law Journal,* Summer 2007.

Jaksic, Vesna. "Guidelines for Outsourcing Grow," *The National Law Journal,* May 3, 2007.

Jones, Leigh. "A Grim Verdict Awaits Law Grads," *The National Law Journal,* October 20, 2008.

Jones, Leigh. "Latest Associate Pay Hikes Leave Corporate Clients Cold," *The National Law Journal*, August 13, 2007.

Karkaria, Urvakesh. "Shipping Legal Work Overseas," *Atlanta Business Chronicle,* August 29, 2008.

King, Rachel. "Outsourcing: Beyond Bangalore," *Business Week Online,* December 11, 2006.

Koppel, Nathan. "Recession Batters Law Firms, Triggering Layoffs, Closings," *The Wall Street Journal*, January 26, 2009.

Krebsbach, Karen. "Inside the Outsourcing World of India," *Bank Technology News*, January 1, 2007.

Krishnan, Jayanth K. "Outsourcing and the Globalizing Legal Profession," *William and Mary Law Review,* May 2007.

Leone, Marie. "From Inside Counsel to Offshore Counsel?" *CFO.com,* October 7, 2005.

Lin, Anthony. "ABA Gives Thumbs Up to Legal Outsourcing," *New York Law Journal,* August 27, 2008.

Lloyd, Richard. "British Firms Watch Australia's Law Firm IPOs with Interest," *The American Lawyer,* June 6, 2007.

Malan, Douglas S. "Ex-litigator Founds Fresh Web Resource," *The Connecticut Law Tribune,* March 11, 2008.

Maleski, Melissa and Christopher Danzig. "Salary Slump," *Inside Counsel*, January 1, 2009.

Meyer, Gene. "Without Lawyer's Help: Companies See Potential Sales in Do-It-Yourself Legal Kits," *Orlando Sentinel,* January 20, 2008.

Middlemiss, Jim. "Contract with India: Legal Outsourcing," *Financial Post*, April 25, 2008.

Mishra, Pankaj. "It's a Round World After All: India, China, and the Global Economy," *Harper's Magazine*, August 2007.

Morrison, Rees W. "Managerial Opportunities Presented by Commodity Legal Work," *Texas Lawyer*, Vol. 23, No. 17, July 2, 2007.

Mountain, Darryl R. "Disrupting Conventional Law Firm Business Models Using Document Assembly," *International Journal of Law and Information Technology*, Summer 2007.

Neil, Martha. "General Counsel Leaves Merrill Lynch (Corrected)," *ABAJournal.com*, January 31, 2009.

Neil, Martha. "Going Public Pays: 56% Profit Increase Follows Law Firm's IPO," *ABAJournal.com*, February 22, 2008.

Neil, Martha. "January's Carnage: 1,487 Law Layoffs," *ABAJournal.com*, January 29, 2009.

Norman, Forrest. "Attorneys from Miami, Chicago Band Together to Bring Controversial Practice of Legal Outsourcing to South Florida," *Broward Daily Business Review*, February 21, 2007.

Owens, Laura Lewis. "With Legal Services, World is Flat: Savvy Consumers Know the Best Tool Belt Carries Many Tools, and Will Seek the Right One for the Job," *The National Law Journal*, January 15, 2007.

Passarella, Gina. "Higher Profits, Revenues for Stevens & Lee: Firm's Unique Accounting Model Places Emphasis on Net Income per Lawyer," *Legal Intelligencer*, Vol. 235, No. 49, March 13, 2007.

Passarella, Gina. "Is the Work-Life Balance Tipping in Work's Favor?" *The Legal Intelligencer*, February 5, 2009.

Passarella, Gina. "Law Department Budget Cuts Could Lead to Change in Outside Firms," *The Legal Intelligencer*, December 12, 2008.

Patel, Mehul. "Ecosystem of Legal Services is Evolving," *The National Law Journal*, May 1, 2008.

Press, Aric. "In-house: The Lateral Report: A Record Number of *AmLaw* 100 and 200 Partners Changed Firms Last Year," *The American Lawyer*, February 1, 2009.

Price, Marie. "More Law Firms Focus Recruiting Efforts on Specialized Fields," *Journal Record*, January 22, 2008.

Ramstack, Tom. "Law Firms Send Case Work Overseas to Boost Efficiency," *The Washington Times*, September 26, 2005.

Ribeiro, John. "Customers Looking Beyond India for Outsourcing," *InfoWorld Daily*, November 7, 2007.

Royal, Amanda. "800 Law Firm Jobs Lost in One Day," *The Recorder,* February 13, 2009.

Russell, George W. "In-house or Outsourced? The Future of Corporate Counsel," *Asia Law,* July/August 2005.

Sachdev, Ameet. "Much Shelist Makes a Case for Small, Independent Firms," *Chicago Tribune,* October 30, 2007.

Sager, Thomas. "Bigger Isn't Better," *Law Firm Inc.,* Vol. 5, Issue 2, March 2007.

Sherman, Ann. "Should Small Firms Get on Board with Outsourcing?" *Small Firm Business,* September 12, 2005.

Sileo, Carmel. "More States Putting A La Carte Legal Services on the Menu," *Trial,* March 2007.

Slater, Dan. "Big-Law Associates Facing 2008 Salary Cap," *WSJ.com,* February 15, 2008.

Sloan, Karen. "Declining Law Firm Profits Forecast for '09," *The National Law Journal,* February 3, 2009.

Sloan, Karen and Drew Combs. "O'Melveny Cuts 200 Attorneys, Staff; Dewey, Shearman Cut Support Staff," *The National Law Journal,* March 4, 2009.

Sloan, Karen, "Survey: Most Attorneys Working Part-Time Are Women," *The National Law Journal,* December 31, 2008.

Sloan, Karen. "The View from 3L: Law Students Brace for Tough Reality," *The National Law Journal,* January 26, 2009.

Smith, Rich. "A Passage to India," *The Motley Fool,* January 26, 2004.

Stephey, M.J. "Gen-X: The Ignored Generation?" *Time Magazine,* April 16, 2008.

Sterling, John. "Mid-size Law Firms: What Are They Today, and Are They Really Doomed?" *Of Counsel,* August 2007.

Tejaswi, Mini Joseph. "Hollywood's Legal Work is Done in Mysore," *The Times of India,* November 13, 2007.

Thomas, Molly. "Snap Judgments," *Business Law Today,* September/October 2007.

Usellis, Mark. "Resisting the Urge to Merge," *Legal Management,* November/December 2006.

VanWormer, Nina Ingwer. "Help at Your Fingertips: A Twenty-first Century Response to the Pro Se Phenomenon," *Vanderbilt Law Review,* April 2007.

Von Nordenflycht, Andrew. "Lawyers Incorporated?" *Financial Post,* January 20, 2009.

Wadhwa, Vivek. "Why Small Tech Companies Aren't Outsourcing," *Business Week Online*, July 23, 2007.

Weier, Mary Hayes. "Get a Grip: As Offshore Outsourcing Heads into its Second Decade, It's Bringing New Risks and Requiring New Strategies," *Information Week*, November 5, 2007.

Wesemann, Ed. "Co-managing Partners Are Worth a Second Look," *Of Counsel*, October 2007.

Williams, Alex. "The Falling-down Professions," the *New York Times*, January 6, 2008.

Winings, Matthew S. "The Power of Law Firm Partnership: Why Dominant Rainmakers Will Impede the Immediate Widespread Implementation of an Autocratic Management Structure," *Drake Law Review*, Fall 2006.

Yates, Bob. "Change: Lawyers and Clients Demand a New Type of Firm," *Chicago Lawyer*, Vol. 30, No. 5, May 2007.

ABA Reports and Ethics Opinions

American Bar Association. "Lawyer's Obligations When Outsourcing Legal and Nonlegal Support Services," *Formal Ethics Opinion 08-451*, American Bar Association Standing Committee on Ethics and Professional Responsibility, August 25, 2008.

American Bar Association. "Surcharge to Client for Use of a Contract Lawyer," *Formal Ethics Opinion 00-420*, American Bar Association Standing Committee on Ethics and Professional Responsibility, November 29, 2000.

American Bar Association. "Temporary Lawyers," *Formal Ethics Opinion 88-356*, American Bar Association Standing Committee on Ethics and Professional Responsibility, December 16, 1988.

Kelly, Anastasia D. and Jeffrey F. Liss, et al. "The ABA Commission on Billable Hours Report," the ABA Commission on Billable Hours, August 2002.

Surveys, Data & Trends

ABA Lawyer Demographics, ABA Market Research Department.

Altman Weil, Inc. "Chief Legal Officer Survey," 2008.

Altman Weil, Inc. "Flash Survey on the Diversity Manager Position in Large Law Firms," January 2007.

Altman Weil, Inc. "Law Department Cost Control: A Flash Survey of General Counsel," January 17, 2009.

Altman Weil, Inc. "Law Department Metrics Benchmarking Survey," 2007.

Altman Weil, Inc. "Law Department Metrics Benchmarking Survey," 2006.

Altman Weil, Inc. "Survey of Major Law Firm Management Techniques," July 2005.

Berman, Jay M. "Industry Output and Employment Projections to 2014," *Monthly Labor Review,* Bureau of Labor Statistics, November 2005.

Bernstein, Robert and Tom Edwards. "An Older and More Diverse Nation by Midcentury," press release from U.S. Census Bureau, August 14, 2008.

Datamonitor. *Legal Services: Global Industry Guide*, 2006.

Essandohn, Virginia Grant. "Good Housekeeping: the Law Firm Diversity Assessment," *Report to Legal Management,* Altman Weil, Inc., May 2007.

Forrester Research. "North America Technographics Benchmark Survey," 2008.

Gavin, Jamie. "Global Internet Audience Surpasses 1 Billion Visitors," comScore Press Release, January 23, 2009.

Gordon, Kimberly. "Law Firm Mergers Continue Upward Trend in 2009," Hildebrandt International, Press Release, January 2009.

Handwerk, Phil. "National Applicant Trends—2007," Law School Admission Council, Inc., 2008.

Hildebrandt International, Citi Private Bank. "Client Advisory," January 2009.

Hildebrandt International. "Law Department Survey," 2008.

Incisive Legal Intelligence. "*The National Law Journal* Staffing Survey of the *NLJ* 250 law firms," 2008.

International Monetary Fund. "World Growth Grinds to Virtual Halt, IMF Urges Decisive Global Policy Response," *World Economic Outlook,* January 2009.

NALP. "How Much Do Law Firms Pay New Associates? A 12-year Retrospective as Reported by Firms," NALP *Bulletin*, October 2007.

NALP. "Law Firm Leverage Varied with Firm Size and Location in 2006," NALP *Bulletin*, January 18, 2007.

NALP. "Market for New Law Graduates at Highest Level in 20 Years, Approaching 92%," *Class of 2007 Selected Findings,* NALP Survey & Press Release, July 24, 2008.

NALP. "How Much Do Associates Have to Work?" NALP *Bulletin*, April 2007.

NALP. "Minority Women Still Underrepresented in Law Firm
Partnership Ranks—Change in Diversity of Law Firm Leadership
Very Slow Overall," NALP Press Release, November 1, 2007.

NALP. "Salaries at Largest Firms Continue to Rise Rapidly," *2007
Associate Salary Survey,* January 14, 2007.

Snyder, Scott, et al. *Legal Transformation Study: Your 2020 Vision of the
Future*, Minnesota: Decision Strategies International and Legal
Research Center, 2008.

ValueNotes. "The BPO Industry: Trends 2009," January 14, 2009.

VAULT/Minority Corporate Counsel Association Guide to Law Firm
Diversity Programs, 2007.

Wilber, James. "Legal Profession Trends and Outlook," *Report to Legal
Management*, Altman Weil, Inc., February 2007.

Websites

Altman Weil, Inc.: www.altmanweil.com

American Bar Association: www.abanet.org

American Lawyer: www.americanlawyer.com

Association of Corporate Counsel: www.acc.com

Bureau of Labor Statistics, United States Department of Labor:
www.bls.gov

Forrester Research: www.forrester.com

Hildebrandt International: www.hildebrandt.com

Incisive Legal Intelligence: www.incisivelegalintel.com

Lumen Legal: www.lumenlegal.com

NALP: www.nalp.org

The National Law Journal: www.nlj.com

U.S. Census Bureau: www.census.gov

Acknowledgements

To my wife Lynn, who has always been my biggest supporter, has fueled my entrepreneurial dreams, and was the inspiration for this book project.

To my daughter Sarah, who brings great joy to my life every day, through her curiosity, her infectious laugh, but most of all through the unconditional love we share for each other.

To my parents Richard and Suzanne, who serve as great role models for me as a spouse and parent, who introduced me at an early age to the world of entrepreneurship, and who have always been there to lend their support and encouragement to all my endeavors.

To my older brother Paul, an extraordinary friend, teacher, coach and mentor, not only to me but to the thousands of students he has coached and taught over the years. Without doubt, the most entrepreneurial teacher on the planet.

To my business partner Mark Adams, for your ongoing support and commitment to Lumen and your dedication to reshaping the legal industry landscape.

To the Entrepreneurs' Organization, the EO Global Board & Staff, EO Detroit Chapter and my EO Forum group. Our shared passion for helping entrepreneurs reshape the world for the betterment of all drives me on a daily basis to engage leading entrepreneurs to learn and grow. For that, I am forever grateful.

To the Lumen Legal team, thanks for embracing the ideals of Thomas Edison to inspire innovation; for your capacity to constantly change to better serve our clients, candidates and employees; and for living our core values on a daily basis.

Finally, to my writing partner David Barringer, who had an incredibly unique ability to shape my spoken words and visions into great written prose, who tirelessly researched the latest legal industry statistics and events, and who made writing this book a fun and adventuresome journey.

—David Galbenski

A Note on the Project

This book was a two-year collaboration between two Davids. David Galbenski conceived the project, defined the trends, and edited many drafts, while David Barringer organized, wrote, and designed the book. The project changed as the global marketplace changed, especially during 2008 and early 2009. In the end, the intent of the authors was not to present an exhaustive portrait of a still landscape but to explore overarching trends in a fast-moving world. In the next few years, there will surely be remarkable developments to add to a revised edition.

About David Galbenski

David Galbenski is President and CEO of Lumen Legal. He is also Chairman of the Global Board of Directors of the Entrepreneurs' Organization (EO), which has over 7,000 members in thirty-eight countries.

David graduated with distinction from the University of Michigan Business School in 1990 and *cum laude* from Wayne State University Law School in 1993. In 1993, David had the idea for Lumen Legal while practicing as a commercial litigation associate for the Detroit law firm of Timmis and Inman. After a futile search for a source for contract staff to give his firm the document-review capability it needed, he developed the concept for a contract-staffing firm that would focus solely on legal professionals. David and partner Mark Adams funded the start-up, and the company has enjoyed fast growth through the 1990s and into this century.

Lumen is a two-time recipient of the *Inc.* 500 award as one of America's fastest growing, privately-held companies. David received the prestigious Ernst & Young Entrepreneur of the Year Award in 2005 for the Staffing & IT Consulting Services category for the Central Great Lakes region. David is proud of developing an employee-centric culture at Lumen that embraces innovation. As a result, Lumen has consistently been recognized as one of the best companies to work for in Michigan over the past several years. David and his company have been featured in *The Wall Street Journal, Entrepreneur, Business Week, Law Practice Today, Journal of Legal Marketing, Crain's Detroit Business, LPO Watch, National Law Journal, Legal Management,* and *Small Firm Business.*

About Lumen Legal

Lumen Legal is a privately held, entrepreneur-driven company. A global team of attorneys, paralegals, and consulting and staffing-industry professionals, Lumen Legal provides corporations and law firms with custom legal-service solutions that raise efficiency, reduce costs, preserve quality, and drive business success. The company excels at matching global and disparate resources to meet demanding client needs. In short, Lumen Legal is an engine driving dramatic change in the legal-service industry.

About David Barringer

David Barringer is a freelance writer, novelist, and graphic designer. He is the author of the books of design criticism *There's Nothing Funny about Design* (Princeton Architectural Press, 2009) and *American Mutt Barks in the Yard* (Emigre, 2005) and the novels *American Home Life* (So New Publishing, 2007) and *Johnny Red* (Word Riot Press, 2005). He graduated from the University of Michigan (1991) and the University of Michigan Law School (1995). He has written for *The American Bar Association Journal, I.D. Magazine,* the *New York Times Book Review, The American Prospect, Details, The Detroit Free Press,* and many others. He is the winner of the 2008 Winterhouse Award for Design Writing and Criticism. Contact him at dlbarringer@gmail.com and at www.davidbarringer.com.